Rabbi Nachman's

# Tikun HaKlali

Rabbi Nachman's

# Tikun HaKlali

A Direct Translation

by

Daniel A. Elias

Tzeruf Co

Author: *Daniel A. Elias, J.D.*

Publisher:                          Tzeruf Co
                                235 S Lyon Ave #39
                              Hemet, CA  92543      USA
                                   mail@tzeruf.com

SAN Number                              853-0203

© 2012 by Tzeruf Co.
Printed in USA

First Edition Published 2013

**Publisher's Cataloging-in-Publication data**

Elias, Daniel A..

Tzeruf Basics; a Kabbalah Meditation.    illustrated by Daniel Elias.
p. cm.
Includes index.

English Paperback    ISBN 978-0-9792826-3-8

1. Religion 2. Bible. 3. Meditation. 4. Hebrew. I. Title.

Dedication:

I dedicate this book to

Rabbi Abraham Nachman, ben Simcha

Rabbi Nachman believed this
Tikun Ha Klali to be one of his life-
time accomplishments......

"When my days are ended and I leave this world, I will intercede for anyone who....says these Ten Psalms, and gives to charity. No matter how serious his sins and transgressions, I will do everything in my power to save him and cleanse him. I will go to the end of the Creation for him. By his hair I will pull him out of Gehennom!"

-- Rabbi Nachman, *Tikun Ha Klali*

# TABLE OF CONTENTS

**Translations.** The objective of the translated Hebrew in this book is;

1) to help one to be fluent in the reading of Hebrew,

2) to learn Hebrew vocabulary by seeing directly below the Hebrew word what the English translation is.

3) to memorize parts of the verses of the sacred scriptures

4) to easily increase kavanah or thought intension when praying the Psalms.

5) to feed the soul the effects of bible code while reading the biblical verses

One translated Hebrew word of a verse contains so much subtle information. There is the root, the prefix, the affix, dropped weak letters, gutturals, dagesh lene, dagesh forte, it's sentence grammatical name, etc. Much of the english grammar has been left out by necessity; ie. the translation "the" was put in only when there was a specific prefix letter Heh, not where a prefix has a patach.

Every expression in the [ongoing] present tense can variably be expressed in the future tense as well as in the past tense because anything that is ongoing in the present tense has already happened and will continue to happen.

I would have preferred to translate the tenses of the verbs as they actually appear instead of looking to the sentence meaning to infer the past, present or future. This best reflects the base thought of Hebrew language. However in order to make the text as simple to understand for the majority of people who do not understand this concept I have put in the inferred verb tenses.

# INTRO TO TIKUN HAKLALI

Rebbi Nachman stated that this tikun was one of his best accomplishments. He was very pleased that he was able to discover a general rectification, or general remedy. He called it the Global Remedy. Every negative experience has its own remedy, but the Tikkun HaKlali is the Complete Remedy. This remedy consists of ten psalms specifically chosen by Rebbi Nachman. The ten Tikun HaKlali Psalms are 16, 32, 41, 42, 59, 77, 90, 105, 137, and 150. They have the power to nullify the strength of the klipah, negative forces, and any blemish of a negative experience.

The Tikun should be said by those seeking a remedy for any problem they might be experiencing. It should be said in sequence as a whole, and uninterrupted.

Rebbi Nachman said, "If someone comes to my grave, gives a coin to charity, and says these ten Psalms [the Tikkun HaKlali], I will pull him out from the depths of Gehinnom!" (Rabbi Nachman's Wisdom #141). "It makes no difference what he did until that day, but from that day on, he must take upon himself not to return to his foolish ways".

## Dedication

Rabbi Nachman stated that making dedication to a pious deceased tzadik (righteous man) was most important to do. The reason is because the pious tzadik who have passed away to another dimension will best put to use the prayers one says. Then when the person praying needs help the most, that is when the deceased sage will help him or her the most.

## Psalm 119

Psalm 119 was included because it was said everyday by Rabbi Nachman's grandfather, the Baal Shem Tov. The Baal Shem Tov stated that if this Psalm 119 is said everyday, a person will be able to enter into a meditative state when talking to another and receive deep perceptions about that person.

Set aside tzadaka (charity ) now.

## DEDICATION

הֲרֵינִי מְקַשֵּׁר עַצְמִי לְמִיזְמוֹרִים אֵלֶא

| here I | attach | myself | to psalms | these |
|---|---|---|---|---|

לְרַבֵּנוּ נַחְמָן בֶּן פֵיגֶא

| to our rabbi | Nachman | son | Feige |
|---|---|---|---|

וּלְכָל הַצַּדִיקִים שֶׁבְדוֹרֵנוּ

| to all | the pious ones | that in our generation |
|---|---|---|

וּלְכָל הַצַּדִיקִים כִּי אֶל־עָפָר שָׁבוּ׃

| and to all | the pious ones | like | dust - unto | they returned |
|---|---|---|---|---|

# PSALM 16

ספר תהילים פרק טז

מִכְתָּם לְדָוִד שָׁמְרֵנִי אֵל כִּי־חָסִיתִי בָךְ:

| in you | I take refuge - like | El | heed me | to David | inscription |

1. A Miktam of David. Preserve me, O God; for in you I put my trust.

אָמַרְתְּ לַיהוָה אֲדֹנָי אָתָּה טוֹבָתִי בַּל־עָלֶיךָ:

| upon you - in not | my goodness | you | Adoni | to ihvh | I said |

2. I have said to the Lord, You are my Lord; I have no good apart from you;

לִקְדוֹשִׁים אֲשֶׁר־בָּאָרֶץ הֵמָּה וְאַדִּירֵי כָּל־חֶפְצִי־בָם:

| in them – my delighting – all | and nobel ones | they are | in earth -which | to holy ones |

3. As for the holy ones who are in the earth, they are the excellent, in whom is all my delight.

יִרְבּוּ עַצְּבוֹתָם אַחֵר מָהָרוּ

| they rush | seeking another (god) | their sorrows | they increase |

בַּל־אַסִּיךְ נִסְכֵּיהֶם מִדָּם

| from blood | their libations | I libate – in not |

וּבַל־אֶשָּׂא אֶת־שְׁמוֹתָם עַל־שְׂפָתָי:

| my lips – upon | their names - that | I lift - and in not |

4. And for those who choose another god, their sorrows shall be multiplied; their drink offerings of blood I will not offer, nor take up their names upon my lips.

יְהוָה מְנָת־חֶלְקִי וְכוֹסִי אַתָּה תּוֹמִיךְ גּוֹרָלִי:

| my lot | you maintain | you | and my glass | my portion – alloting | ihvh |

5. The Lord is the portion of my inheritance and of my cup; you maintain my lot.

חֲבָלִים נָפְלוּ־לִי בַּנְּעִמִים אַף־נַחֲלָת שָׁפְרָה עָלָי:

| upon me | towards beautiful | portion - then | in pleasant ones | to me – they fallen | lines |

6. The lines are fallen for me in pleasant places; I have a goodly heritage.

אֲבָרֵךְ אֶת־יְהוָה אֲשֶׁר יְעָצָנִי

| counsels me | which | ihvh – that | I bless |

אַף־לֵילוֹת יִסְּרוּנִי כִלְיוֹתָי:

| like night seasons | they disciplins me | nights - then |

7. I will bless the Lord, who has given me counsel; my insides also instruct me in the night seasons.

שִׁוִּיתִי יְהוָה לְנֶגְדִּי תָמִיד כִּי מִימִינִי בַּל־אֶמּוֹט:

<small>I will slip - in not   from my right hand   like   always   to before me   ihvh   I have set</small>

8. I have set the Lord always before me; because he is at my right hand, I shall not be moved.

לָכֵן שָׂמַח לִבִּי וַיָּגֶל כְּבוֹדִי אַף־בְּשָׂרִי יִשְׁכֹּן לָבֶטַח:

<small>to safety   it tabernacle   my flesh - then   my honor   and rejoiced   my heart   happy   to thus</small>

9. Therefore my heart is glad, and my glory rejoices; my flesh also dwells secure.

כִּי לֹא־תַעֲזֹב נַפְשִׁי לִשְׁאוֹל

<small>to Shoel   my soul   you abandon - not   like</small>

לֹא־תִתֵּן חֲסִידְךָ לִרְאוֹת שָׁחַת:

<small>pit   to seeings   your pious one   you give - not</small>

10. (K) For you will not abandon my soul to Sheol; nor will you suffer your pious one to see the pit.

תּוֹדִיעֵנִי אֹרַח חַיִּים

<small>life   path   you make me know</small>

שֹׂבַע שְׂמָחוֹת אֶת־פָּנֶיךָ נְעִמוֹת בִּימִינְךָ נֶצַח:

<small>victory   in your right hand   pleasures   your presence – that   happinesses   full</small>

11. You will show me the path of life; in your presence is fullness of joy; at your right hand there are pleasures for evermore.

## PSALM 32

ספר תהילים פרק לב

לְדָוִד מַשְׂכִּיל אַשְׁרֵי נְשׂוּי־פֶּשַׁע כְּסוּי חֲטָאָה:

sin   covered   transgression - lifted   happy   contemplation   to David

1. A Psalm of David, A Maskil. Happy is he whose transgression is forgiven, whose sin is covered.

אַשְׁרֵי אָדָם לֹא יַחְשֹׁב יְהוָֹה לוֹ עָוֹן

inequity   to him   ihvh   he reconing   not   Adam   happy

וְאֵין בְּרוּחוֹ רְמִיָּה:

deceit   in his spirit   and isn't

2. Happy is the man to whom the Lord does not impute iniquity, and in whose spirit there is no guile.

כִּי הֶחֱרַשְׁתִּי בָּלוּ עֲצָמָי בְּשַׁאֲגָתִי כָּל־הַיּוֹם:

the day – all   in my roaring   my bones   deteriorated   the my silence   like

3. When I kept silence, my bones wasted away through my groaning all day long.

כִּי יוֹמָם וָלַיְלָה תִּכְבַּד עָלַי יָדֶךָ

your hand   upon me   you heavy   and night   by day   like

נֶהְפַּךְ לְשַׁדִּי בְּחַרְבֹנֵי קַיִץ סֶלָה:

interlude   summer   into droughts   my freshness   changed

4. For day and night your hand was heavy on me; my moisture is turned into the drought of summer. Selah.

חַטָּאתִי אוֹדִיעֲךָ וַעֲוֹנִי לֹא־כִסִּיתִי

I covered – not   and my inequity   I acknowledge you   my sin

אָמַרְתִּי אוֹדֶה עֲלֵי פְשָׁעַי לַיהוָֹה

to ihvh   my transgressions   upon me   I will acknowledge   I said

וְאַתָּה נָשָׂאתָ עֲוֹן חַטָּאתִי סֶלָה:

interlude   my sin   inequity   you lifted   and you

5. I acknowledged my sin to you, and I did not hide my iniquity. I said, I will confess my transgressions to the Lord; and you forgave the iniquity of my sin. Selah.

עַל־זֹאת יִתְפַּלֵּל כָּל־חָסִיד אֵלֶיךָ לְעֵת מְצֹא

found   to time   unto you   righteous – all   he prays   this - upon

רַק לְשֵׁטֶף מַיִם רַבִּים אֵלָיו לֹא יַגִּיעוּ:

| only | to flood | waters | many ones | unto him | not | they will touch |
|------|----------|--------|-----------|----------|-----|-----------------|

6. For this shall every one who is pious pray to you in a time when you may be found; then surely the floods of great waters shall not come near him.

אַתָּה סֵתֶר לִי מִצַּר תִּצְּרֵנִי

| you | hiding place | to me | from trouble | you preserve me |
|-----|--------------|-------|--------------|-----------------|

רָנֵּי פַלֵּט תְּסוֹבְבֵנִי סֶלָה:

| my joy shouting | deliverance | you surround me | interlude |
|-----------------|-------------|-----------------|-----------|

7. You are my hiding place; you shall preserve me from trouble; you shall surround me with songs of deliverance. Selah.

אַשְׂכִּילְךָ וְאוֹרְךָ בְּדֶרֶךְ־זוּ תֵלֵךְ אִיעֲצָה עָלֶיךָ עֵינִי:

| I will contemplate you | and direct you | I will counsel | you walk | this – in way | upon you | I will counsel | my eyes |
|------------------------|----------------|----------------|----------|---------------|----------|----------------|---------|

8. I will instruct you and teach you in the way which you shall go; I will counsel you with my eye upon you.

אַל־תִּהְיוּ כְּסוּס כְּפֶרֶד אֵין הָבִין

| you be - don't | like horse | like mule | isn't | the understanding |
|----------------|------------|-----------|-------|-------------------|

בְּמֶתֶג וָרֶסֶן עֶדְיוֹ לִבְלוֹם בַּל קְרֹב אֵלֶיךָ:

| in bit | and bridle | his ornament | to restrain | without | near | unto you |
|--------|------------|--------------|-------------|----------|------|----------|

9. Do not be like the horse, or like the mule, which have no understanding; whose mouth must be held in with bit and bridle, lest they do not come near you.

רַבִּים מַכְאוֹבִים לָרָשָׁע וְהַבּוֹטֵחַ בַּיהֹוָה חֶסֶד יְסוֹבְבֶנּוּ:

| many ones | pain ones | to wicked | and the truster | in ihvh | kindness | it surrounds him |
|-----------|-----------|-----------|-----------------|---------|----------|------------------|

10. Many are the sorrows of the wicked; but loving kindness shall surround him who trusts in the Lord.

שִׂמְחוּ בַיהֹוָה וְגִילוּ צַדִּיקִים וְהַרְנִינוּ כָּל־יִשְׁרֵי־לֵב:

| you happy | in ihvh | and you rejoice | righteous ones | and the joy shout | heart – upright ones– all |
|-----------|---------|-----------------|----------------|-------------------|---------------------------|

11. Be glad in the Lord, and rejoice, you righteous; and shout for joy, all you who are upright in heart.

# PSALM 41

לַמְנַצֵּחַ　　מִזְמוֹר　לְדָוִד:

to one making permanent　Psalm　to David

1. To the chief Musician, A Psalm of David.

אַשְׁרֵי　מַשְׂכִּיל　אֶל־דָּל　בְּיוֹם　רָעָה　יְמַלְּטֵהוּ　יְהוָה:

happy　applys intelligence　poor - unto　in day　evil　he will make escape you　ihvh

2. Happy is he who considers the poor; the Lord will save in the day of evil.

יְהוָה　יִשְׁמְרֵהוּ　וִיחַיֵּהוּ　יְאֻשַּׁר [וְאֻשַּׁר]　בָּאָרֶץ

ihvh　he will heed you　and he enliven you　and make happy　in earth

וְאַל־תִּתְּנֵהוּ　בְּנֶפֶשׁ　אֹיְבָיו:

you give it - and don't　in soul　his enemies

3. (K) The Lord will preserve him, and keep him alive; he is called happy on earth; and you will not deliver him to the will of his enemies.

יְהוָה　יִסְעָדֶנּוּ　עַל־עֶרֶשׂ　דְּוָי　כָּל־מִשְׁכָּבוֹ　הָפַכְתָּ　בְחָלְיוֹ:

ihvh　he will brace him　couch - upon　languishing　his bed - all　you restore　in his illness

4. The Lord will strengthen him on his sick bed; whenever he is prostrate you will heal all his illnesses.

אֲנִי־אָמַרְתִּי　יְהוָה　חָנֵּנִי　רְפָאָה　נַפְשִׁי　כִּי־חָטָאתִי　לָךְ:

I said - I　ihvh　grant me　heal　my soul　I sinned - like　to you

5. I said, Lord, be merciful to me; heal my soul; for I have sinned against you.

אוֹיְבַי　יֹאמְרוּ　רַע　לִי　מָתַי　יָמוּת　וְאָבַד　שְׁמוֹ:

my enemies　they say　bad　to me　when　he will die　and perish　his name

6. My enemies speak evil of me, When shall he die, and his name perish?

וְאִם־בָּא　לִרְאוֹת　שָׁוְא　יְדַבֵּר

come - and if　to see　vanity　he speaks

לִבּוֹ　יִקְבָּץ־אָוֶן　לוֹ　יֵצֵא　לַחוּץ　יְדַבֵּר:

his heart　inequity - he gathers　to him　goes out　to outside　he speaks

7. And if one comes to see me, he speaks vanity; his heart gathers iniquity to itself; when he goes out, he tells it.

יַחַד　עָלַי　יִתְלַחֲשׁוּ　כָּל־שֹׂנְאָי　עָלַי　יַחְשְׁבוּ　רָעָה　לִי:

together　upon me　they whisper　haters of me - all　upon me　they devise　evil　to me

8. All who hate me whisper together against me; against me they plot my harm.

דְּבַר־בְּלִיַּעַל יָצוּק בּוֹ וַאֲשֶׁר שָׁכַב לֹא־יוֹסִיף לָקוּם:

to rise   he again - not   he lyes   and which   in it   it pours out   in decadence - speaking

9. They say, An evil disease cleaves fast to him, and from where he lies he shall rise up no more.

גַּם אִישׁ־שְׁלוֹמִי אֲשֶׁר־בָּטַחְתִּי בוֹ

in him   I trusted – which   my peaceful one – man   also

אוֹכֵל לַחְמִי הִגְדִּיל עָלַי עָקֵב:

heel   upon me   cased to make great   my bread   eater

10. Even my own close friend, in whom I trusted, who ate of my bread, has lifted up his heel against me.

וְאַתָּה יְהוָה חָנֵּנִי וַהֲקִימֵנִי וַאֲשַׁלְּמָה לָהֶם:

to them   and I will pay   and the raise me up   grant me   ihvh   and you

11. But you, O Lord, be gracious to me, and raise me up, that I may pay them back.

בְּזֹאת יָדַעְתִּי כִּי־חָפַצְתָּ בִּי כִּי לֹא־יָרִיעַ אֹיְבִי עָלָי:

upon me   my enemy   he joy shouting – not   like   in me   you favor – like   I know   in this

12. By this I know that you favor me, because my enemy does not triumph over me.

וַאֲנִי בְּתֻמִּי תָּמַכְתָּ בִּי וַתַּצִּיבֵנִי לְפָנֶיךָ לְעוֹלָם:

forever   before you   you station me   in me   you supported   in my integrity   and I

13. And as for me, you uphold me in my integrity, and you set me before your face for ever.

בָּרוּךְ יְהוָה אֱלֹהֵי יִשְׂרָאֵל

Israel   Elohim of   ihvh   blessed

מֵהָעוֹלָם וְעַד הָעוֹלָם אָמֵן וְאָמֵן:

and amen   amen   the forever   and till   from the forever

14. Blessed be the Lord God of Israel from everlasting, and to everlasting. Amen, and Amen.

# PSALM 42

ספר תהילים פרק מב

לַמְנַצֵּחַ     מַשְׂכִּיל     לִבְנֵי־קֹרַח:
to one making permanent    contemplation    Korah - to sons

1. To the chief Musician, A Maskil, for the sons of Korah.

כְּאַיָּל     תַּעֲרֹג     עַל־אֲפִיקֵי־מָיִם
like the male deer    it pants    water – brooks – upon

כֵּן נַפְשִׁי תַעֲרֹג אֵלֶיךָ אֱלֹהִים:
thus    my soul    it pants    unto you    Elohim

2. As the hart longs for water streams, so does my soul long for you, O God.

צָמְאָה נַפְשִׁי לֵאלֹהִים לְאֵל חָי
thirsts    my soul    to Elohim    to El    living

מָתַי אָבוֹא וְאֵרָאֶה פְּנֵי אֱלֹהִים:
when    I come    and I appear    face    Elohim

3. My soul thirsts for God, for the living God; when shall I come and appear
before God?

הָיְתָה־לִּי דִמְעָתִי לֶחֶם יוֹמָם וָלָיְלָה
to me - it was    my tear    bread    by day    and night

בֶּאֱמֹר אֵלַי כָּל־הַיּוֹם אַיֵּה אֱלֹהֶיךָ:
in saying    unto me    the day – all    where    your Elohim

4. My tears have been my bread day and night, while they continually say to
me, Where is your God?

אֵלֶּה אֶזְכְּרָה וְאֶשְׁפְּכָה עָלַי נַפְשִׁי
these    I remember    and I pour out    upon me    my soul

כִּי אֶעֱבֹר בַּסָּךְ אֶדַּדֵּם עַד־בֵּית אֱלֹהִים
like    I pass    in amount    I will wonder them    house – till    Elohim

בְּקוֹל־רִנָּה וְתוֹדָה הָמוֹן חוֹגֵג:
joy shouting - in voice    and thanks    multitude    festivaling

5. When I remember these things, I pour out my soul; how I went with the
multitude, leading them in procession to the house of God, with the voice of
joy and praise, a crowd keeping the festival.

מַה־תִּשְׁתּוֹחֲחִי נַפְשִׁי וַתֶּהֱמִי עָלַי
why - you prostrating    my soul    and clamoring    upon me

הוֹחִילִי לֵאלֹהִים כִּי־עוֹד אוֹדֶנּוּ יְשׁוּעוֹת פָּנָיו:

his faces    salvations    I acclaim him    still – like    to Elohim    my hope

6. Why are you cast down, O my soul? And why are you disquieted within me?
Hope in God; for I shall again praise him for the help of his countenance.

אֱלֹהַי עָלַי נַפְשִׁי תִשְׁתּוֹחָח

it prostrating    my soul    upon me    my Elohim

עַל־כֵּן אֶזְכָּרְךָ מֵאֶרֶץ יַרְדֵּן וְחֶרְמוֹנִים מֵהַר מִצְעָר:

Mizar   from Mountain   and Hermon ones   Jordan   from land   I remember you   thus - upon

7. O my God, my soul is cast down within me, because I remember you from
the land of the Jordan, and the Hermon, from Mount Mizar.

תְּהוֹם אֶל־תְּהוֹם קוֹרֵא לְקוֹל צִנּוֹרֶיךָ

your conduits    to voice    caller    deep – unto    deep

כָּל־מִשְׁבָּרֶיךָ וְגַלֶּיךָ עָלַי עָבָרוּ:

they pass    upon me    and your billows    your waves - all

8. Deep calls to deep at the noise of your cataracts; all your waves and your
billows have gone over me.

יוֹמָם יְצַוֶּה יְהוָה חַסְדּוֹ

his kindness    ihvh    he commands    by day

וּבַלַּיְלָה שִׁירֹה [שִׁירוֹ] עִמִּי תְּפִלָּה לְאֵל חַיָּי:

my life    to El    prayer    with me    his song    and in night

9. By day the Lord will command his loving kindness, and in the night his song
shall be with me, a prayer to the God of my life.

אוֹמְרָה לְאֵל סַלְעִי

my rock cliff    to El    I will say

לָמָה שְׁכַחְתָּנִי לָמָה־קֹדֵר אֵלֵךְ בְּלַחַץ אוֹיֵב:

enemy    in oppression    I go    somber – why    you forgot me    why

10. I will say to God my rock, Why have you forgotten me? Why do I go
mourning because of the oppression of the enemy?

בְּרֶצַח בְּעַצְמוֹתַי חֵרְפוּנִי צוֹרְרָי

my foes    they reproached me    in my bones    in murder

בְּאָמְרָם אֵלַי כָּל־הַיּוֹם אַיֵּה אֱלֹהֶיךָ:

your Elohim    where    the day – all    unto me    in their saying

11. Like a deadly wound in my bones, my enemies taunt me; while they say
daily to me, Where is your God?

מַה־תִּשְׁתּוֹחֲחִי נַפְשִׁי וּמַה־תֶּהֱמִי עָלָי
upon me    you clamoring – what    my soul    you prostrate - what

הוֹחִילִי לֵאלֹהִים כִּי־עוֹד אוֹדֶנּוּ יְשׁוּעֹת פָּנַי וֵאלֹהָי׃
and my Elohim   my face   salvations   I acclaim him   still – like   to Elohim   my hope

12. Why are you cast down, O my soul? And why are you disquieted within me? Hope in God; for I shall again praise him, who is the health of my countenance, and my God.

# PSALM 59

ספר תהילים פרק נט

לַמְנַצֵּחַ        אַל־תַּשְׁחֵת לְדָוִד מִכְתָּם
to one making permanent        you destroy – don't   to David   inscription

בְּשְׁלֹחַ שָׁאוּל וַיִּשְׁמְרוּ אֶת־הַבַּיִת לַהֲמִיתוֹ:
in sending   Saul   and they heeded   the house – that   to the his death

1. To the chief Musician, Altaschith, A Miktam of David; when Saul sent,

הַצִּילֵנִי מֵאֹיְבַי אֱלֹהָי מִמִּתְקוֹמְמַי תְּשַׂגְּבֵנִי:
rescue me   from my enemies   my Elohim   from rising up against me   you make impregnable me

2. **and they watched the house to kill him**. Save me from my enemies, O my God; defend me from those who rise up against me.

הַצִּילֵנִי מִפֹּעֲלֵי אָוֶן וּמֵאַנְשֵׁי דָמִים הוֹשִׁיעֵנִי:
rescue me   from workers   iniquity   and from men   blood ones   save me

3. Save me from the evil doers, and save me from bloody men.

כִּי הִנֵּה אָרְבוּ לְנַפְשִׁי יָגוּרוּ עָלַי עַזִּים
like   here   they lie in wait   to my soul   they stir up   upon me   strong ones

לֹא־פִשְׁעִי וְלֹא־חַטָּאתִי יְהוָה:
my transgression – not   my sin – and not   ihvh

4. For, behold, they lie in wait for my soul; fierce men are gathered against me; not for my transgression, nor for my sin, O Lord.

בְּלִי־עָוֹן יְרוּצוּן וְיִכּוֹנָנוּ עוּרָה לִקְרָאתִי וּרְאֵה:
iniquity – without   they run   and they prepare   arouse   to meet me   and see

5. They run and prepare themselves for no fault of mine; awake to help me, and behold.

וְאַתָּה יְהוָה־אֱלֹהִים צְבָאוֹת אֱלֹהֵי יִשְׂרָאֵל
and you   Elohim – ihvh   hosts   my Elohim   Israel

הָקִיצָה לִפְקֹד כָּל־הַגּוֹיִם
towards awake   to account   the nations – all

אַל־תָּחֹן כָּל־בֹּגְדֵי אָוֶן סֶלָה:
you be gracious – don't   traitors – all   iniquity   interlude

6. You therefore, O Lord God of hosts, the God of Israel, awake to punish all the nations; do not be merciful to any wicked traitors. Selah.

יְשׁוּבוּ לָעֶרֶב יֶהֱמוּ כַכָּלֶב וִיסוֹבְבוּ עִיר:

city   and they go round   like dog   they howl   to evening   they return

7. They return at evening; they howl like dogs, and go prowling around the city.

הִנֵּה יַבִּיעוּן בְּפִיהֶם חֲרָבוֹת בְּשִׂפְתוֹתֵיהֶם כִּי מִי שֹׁמֵעַ:

hearer   who   like   in their lips   swords   in their mouths   they utter   here

8. Behold, they belch out with their mouth; swords are in their lips; for Who hears?, say they.

וְאַתָּה יְהֹוָה תִּשְׂחַק־לָמוֹ תִּלְעַג לְכָל־גּוֹיִם:

nations – to all   you will deride   to them - you will laugh   ihvh   and you

9. But you, O Lord, shall laugh at them; you shall have all the nations in derision.

עֻזּוֹ אֵלֶיךָ אֶשְׁמֹרָה כִּי אֱלֹהִים מִשְׂגַּבִּי:

my fortress   Elohim   like   I will heed   unto you   his strength

10. O my strength, upon you I will wait! For God is my fortress.

אֱלֹהֵי חַסְדּוֹ [חַסְדִּי] יְקַדְּמֵנִי אֱלֹהִים יַרְאֵנִי בְשֹׁרְרָי:

in my lyers in wait   he lets me see   Elohim   he precedes me   my kindness   my Elohim

11. (K) God who loves me shall come to meet me; God shall let me gaze upon my enemies.

אַל־תַּהַרְגֵם פֶּן־יִשְׁכְּחוּ עַמִּי הֲנִיעֵמוֹ בְחֵילְךָ

in your might   the his scatter   my people   they forget - lest   kill them – don't

וְהוֹרִידֵמוֹ מָגִנֵּנוּ אֲדֹנָי:

Adonai   our shield   and his bring down them

12. Do not slay them, lest my people forget; scatter them by your power; and bring them down, O Lord our shield.

חַטַּאת פִּימוֹ דְּבַר־שְׂפָתֵימוֹ וְיִלָּכְדוּ בִגְאוֹנָם

in their arrogance   and they be seized   their lips – speech   their mouth   sin

וּמֵאָלָה וּמִכַּחַשׁ יְסַפֵּרוּ:

they will tell story   and from dissimulation   and from cursing

13. For the sin of their mouth and the words of their lips let them be taken in their arrogance; and for cursing and lying which they speak.

כַּלֵּה בְחֵמָה כַּלֵּה וְאֵינֵמוֹ

and isn't them   finish   in fury   finish

וְיֵדְעוּ כִּי־אֱלֹהִים מֹשֵׁל בְּיַעֲקֹב

in Jacob   ruler   Elohim – like   and you make known

לְאַפְסֵי הָאָרֶץ סֶלָה׃

Sela    the earth    to far ends

14. Consume them in wrath, consume them, till they are no more; and let them know that God rules in Jacob to the ends of the earth. Selah.

וְיָשֻׁבוּ לָעֶרֶב יֶהֱמוּ כַכָּלֶב וִיסוֹבְבוּ עִיר׃

city   and they go round   like dog   they howl   to evening   and they return

15. And at evening let them return; and let them howl like a dog, and go prowling around the city.

הֵמָּה יְנוּעוּן [יְנִיעוּן] לֶאֱכֹל אִם־לֹא יִשְׂבְּעוּ וַיָּלִינוּ׃

and they spend night   they satisfied   not – if   to eat   they wander   they

16. (K) Let them wander up and down for food, and growl if they do not get their fill.

וַאֲנִי אָשִׁיר עֻזֶּךָ וַאֲרַנֵּן לַבֹּקֶר חַסְדֶּךָ

your mercy   to morning   and will I joy shout   your strength   I will sing   and I

כִּי־הָיִיתָ מִשְׂגָּב לִי וּמָנוֹס בְּיוֹם צַר־לִי׃

to me – trouble   in day   and refuge   to me   fortress   you have been – like

17. But I will sing of your power; indeed, I will sing aloud of your loving kindness in the morning; for you have been my fortress and my refuge in the day of my trouble.

עֻזִּי אֵלֶיךָ אֲזַמֵּרָה

I will sing psalms   unto you   my strength

כִּי־אֱלֹהִים מִשְׂגַּבִּי אֱלֹהֵי חַסְדִּי׃

my kindness   my Elohim   my fortress   Elohim - like

18. To you, O my strength, I will sing; for God is my fortress, and the God who loves me.

# PSALM 77

ספר תהילים פרק עז

לַמְנַצֵּחַ　　עַל־יְדִיתוּן [יְדוּתוּן] לְאָסָף מִזְמוֹר׃
to one making permanent – upon Jeduthun to Asaph psalm

1. (K) To the chief Musician, to Jeduthun, A Psalm of Asaph.

קוֹלִי אֶל־אֱלֹהִים
my voice Elohim – unto

וְאֶצְעָקָה קוֹלִי אֶל־אֱלֹהִים　וְהַאֲזִין אֵלָי׃
and I cry my voice Elohim – unto and the give ear unto me

2. I cry aloud to God, aloud to God, that he may hear me.

בְּיוֹם צָרָתִי אֲדֹנָי דָּרָשְׁתִּי יָדִי לַיְלָה נִגְּרָה וְלֹא תָפוּג
in day is slack and not stirring night my hand I sought Adoni my trouble

מֵאֲנָה הִנָּחֵם נַפְשִׁי׃
refuses comfort my soul

3. In the day of my trouble I seek the Lord; my hand is stretched out in the night, and does not rest; my soul refuses to be comforted.

אֶזְכְּרָה אֱלֹהִים וְאֶהֱמָיָה
I remember Elohim and I clamoring

אָשִׂיחָה וְתִתְעַטֵּף רוּחִי סֶלָה׃
I meditate and it faint my spirit Interlude

4. I remember God, and I moan; I meditate and my spirit faints. Selah.

אָחַזְתָּ שְׁמֻרוֹת עֵינָי נִפְעַמְתִּי וְלֹא אֲדַבֵּר׃
you took hold lids my eyes I am agitated and not I speak

5. You hold my eyelids from closing; I am so troubled that I cannot speak.

חִשַּׁבְתִּי יָמִים מִקֶּדֶם שְׁנוֹת עוֹלָמִים׃
I took account the days from old years ancient times

6. I consider the days of old, the years of ancient times.

אֶזְכְּרָה נְגִינָתִי בַּלַּיְלָה עִם־לְבָבִי אָשִׂיחָה וַיְחַפֵּשׂ רוּחִי׃
I remember my melody in night my heart – with I meditate and it searches my spirit

7. I remember my melody in the night; I talk with my heart; and my spirit searches.

הַלְעוֹלָמִים יִזְנַח אֲדֹנָי וְלֹא־יֹסִיף לִרְצוֹת עוֹד׃
the to forevers he cast off Adoni he will add – and not to approve again

8. Will the Lord cast off for ever? And will he be favorable no more?

הֶאָפֵס לָנֶצַח חַסְדּוֹ גָּמַר אֹמֶר לְדֹר וָדֹר:

| the ceased | to victory | his kindness | lapsed | saying | to generation | and generation |

9. Has his loving kindness ceased for ever? Does his promise fail for evermore?

הֲשָׁכַח חַנּוֹת אֵל אִם־קָפַץ בְּאַף רַחֲמָיו סֶלָה:

| the forgotten | graciousness | El | has stopped – if | in anger | his mercies | interlude |

10. Has God forgotten to be gracious? Has he in anger shut up his tender mercies? Selah.

וָאֹמַר חַלּוֹתִי הִיא שְׁנוֹת יְמִין עֶלְיוֹן:

| and I said | my sickness | it | years | right hand | most high |

11. And I said, It is my sickness that the right hand of the Most High has changed.

אֶזְכּוֹר [אֶזְכּוֹר] מַעַלְלֵי־יָהּ כִּי־אֶזְכְּרָה מִקֶּדֶם פִּלְאֶךָ:

| I will remember | Yah - actions | I remember – like | from old | your mystical |

12. (K) I will remember the works of the Lord; surely I will remember your wonders of old.

וְהָגִיתִי בְכָל־פָּעֳלֶךָ וּבַעֲלִילוֹתֶיךָ אָשִׂיחָה:

| and I muse | your works – in all | and in your deeds | I meditate |

13. And I will meditate on all your work, and muse on your deeds.

אֱלֹהִים בַּקֹּדֶשׁ דַּרְכֶּךָ מִי־אֵל גָּדוֹל כֵּאלֹהִים:

| Elohim | in holy place | your way | El – who | great | like Elohim |

14. Your way, O God, is holy. Who is so great a God as our God?

אַתָּה הָאֵל עֹשֵׂה פֶלֶא הוֹדַעְתָּ בָעַמִּים עֻזֶּךָ:

| you | the El | doing | mystical | you make known | in people | your strength |

15. You are the God that does wonders; you have declared your strength among the people.

גָּאַלְתָּ בִּזְרוֹעַ עַמֶּךָ בְּנֵי־יַעֲקֹב וְיוֹסֵף סֶלָה:

| you redeemed | in arm | your people | Jacob – son | and Joseph | interlude |

16. With your arm you have redeemed your people, the sons of Jacob and Joseph. Selah.

רָאוּךָ מַּיִם אֱלֹהִים רָאוּךָ מַּיִם

| they saw you | waters | Elohim | they saw you | waters |

יָחִילוּ אַף יִרְגְּזוּ תְהֹמוֹת:

| they travailed | then | they disturbed | depths |

17. The waters saw you, O God, the waters saw you; they were afraid; the

depths also trembled.

זֹרְמוּ מַיִם עָבוֹת קוֹל נָתְנוּ שְׁחָקִים

| שְׁחָקִים | נָתְנוּ | קוֹל | עָבוֹת | מַיִם | זֹרְמוּ |
|---|---|---|---|---|---|
| skies | they gave | voice | clouds | waters | they stormed |

אַף־חֲצָצֶיךָ יִתְהַלָּכוּ׃

| יִתְהַלָּכוּ | אַף־חֲצָצֶיךָ |
|---|---|
| they go forth | your arrows - then |

18. The clouds poured out water; the skies sent out a sound; your arrows flashed on every side.

קוֹל רַעַמְךָ בַּגַּלְגַּל הֵאִירוּ בְרָקִים תֵּבֵל

| תֵּבֵל | בְרָקִים | הֵאִירוּ | בַּגַּלְגַּל | רַעַמְךָ | קוֹל |
|---|---|---|---|---|---|
| habitations | in lightnings | the lightening it | in whirlwind | your thunder | voice |

רָגְזָה וַתִּרְעַשׁ הָאָרֶץ׃

| הָאָרֶץ | וַתִּרְעַשׁ | רָגְזָה |
|---|---|---|
| the earth | and trembled | disturbed |

19. The voice of your thunder was in the whirlwind; the lightnings lightened the world; the earth trembled and shook.

בַּיָּם דַּרְכֶּךָ וּשְׁבִילְיךָ [וּשְׁבִילְךָ] בְּמַיִם רַבִּים

| רַבִּים | בְּמַיִם | [וּשְׁבִילְךָ] וּשְׁבִילְיךָ | דַּרְכֶּךָ | בַּיָּם |
|---|---|---|---|---|
| great | in waters | and your trails | your way | in sea |

וְעִקְּבוֹתֶיךָ לֹא נֹדָעוּ׃

| נֹדָעוּ | לֹא | וְעִקְּבוֹתֶיךָ |
|---|---|---|
| they known | not | and your footsteps |

20. (K) Your way was through the sea, and your path through the great waters; and your footsteps were not known.

נָחִיתָ כַצֹּאן עַמֶּךָ בְּיַד־מֹשֶׁה וְאַהֲרֹן׃

| וְאַהֲרֹן | בְּיַד־מֹשֶׁה | עַמֶּךָ | כַצֹּאן | נָחִיתָ |
|---|---|---|---|---|
| and Aaron | Moses – in hand | your people | like sheep | you led |

21. You led your people like a flock by the hand of Moses and Aaron.

# PSALM 90

ספר תהילים פרק צ

תְּפִלָּה לְמֹשֶׁה אִישׁ־הָאֱלֹהִים אֲדֹנָי

Adoni　　the Elohim - man　　to Moses　　prayer

מָעוֹן　אַתָּה הָיִיתָ לָּנוּ בְּדֹר וָדֹר:

and generation　in generation　to us　were　you　high dwelling place

1 A Prayer of Moses the man of God. LORD, thou hast been our dwelling place in all generations.

בְּטֶרֶם הָרִים יֻלָּדוּ וַתְּחוֹלֵל אֶרֶץ וְתֵבֵל

and inhabitants　earth　and you fashioned　they born　mountains　in before

וּמֵעוֹלָם עַד־עוֹלָם אַתָּה אֵל:

El　you　forever – until　and from forever

2 Before the mountains were brought forth, or ever thou hadst formed the earth and the world, even from everlasting to everlasting, thou art God.

תָּשֵׁב אֱנוֹשׁ עַד־דַּכָּא וַתֹּאמֶר שׁוּבוּ בְנֵי־אָדָם:

Adam – sons　you return　and you say　crushed – till　mortal man　return

3 Thou turnest man to destruction; and sayest, Return, ye children of men.

כִּי אֶלֶף שָׁנִים בְּעֵינֶיךָ כְּיוֹם אֶתְמוֹל כִּי יַעֲבֹר

it passing　like　yesterday　like day　in your eyes　years　thousand　like

וְאַשְׁמוּרָה בַלָּיְלָה:

in night　and towards I vigil

4 For a thousand years in thy sight are but as yesterday when it is past, and as a watch in the night.

זְרַמְתָּם שֵׁנָה יִהְיוּ בַּבֹּקֶר כֶּחָצִיר יַחֲלֹף:

it sprouts　like short lived grass　in morning　they be　sleep　you storm them

5 Thou carriest them away as with a flood; they are as a sleep: in the morning they are like grass which groweth up.

בַּבֹּקֶר יָצִיץ וְחָלָף לָעֶרֶב יְמוֹלֵל וְיָבֵשׁ:

and it drys out　it cut down　to evening　and sprouts　it blossoms　in morning

6 In the morning it flourisheth, and groweth up; in the evening it is cut down, and withereth.

כִּי־כָלִינוּ בְאַפֶּךָ וּבַחֲמָתְךָ נִבְהָלְנוּ:

we troubled　and in your fury　in your anger　we finished – like

7 For we are consumed by thine anger, and by thy wrath are we troubled.

שַׁתָּ [שַׁתָּה] עֲוֺנֺתֵינוּ לְנֶגְדֶּךָ עֲלֻמֵנוּ לִמְאוֹר פָּנֶיךָ:

<small>your face   to reflect   increase from us   to before you   our inequities   you set</small>

8 Thou hast set our iniquities before thee, our secret sins in the light of thy countenance.

כִּי כָל־יָמֵינוּ פָּנוּ בְעֶבְרָתֶךָ כִּלִּינוּ שָׁנֵינוּ כְמוֹ־הֶגֶה:

<small>musical note – like   our years   we finish   in your rage   they face   our days – all   like</small>

9 For all our days are passed away in thy wrath: we spend our years as a tale that is told.

יְמֵי שְׁנוֹתֵינוּ בָהֶם שִׁבְעִים שָׁנָה

<small>years   seventy   in them   our years   days</small>

וְאִם בִּגְבוּרֺת שְׁמוֹנִים שָׁנָה

<small>years   eighty   in might ones   and if</small>

וְרָהְבָּם עָמָל וָאָוֶן כִּי־גָז חִישׁ וַנָּעֻפָה:

<small>and we fly away   swiftly   sheared – like   and affliction   labor   and their arrogant</small>

10 The days of our years are threescore years and ten; and if by reason of strength they be fourscore years, yet is their strength labour and sorrow; for it is soon cut off, and we fly away.

מִי־יוֹדֵעַ עֺז אַפֶּךָ וּכְיִרְאָתְךָ עֶבְרָתֶךָ:

<small>your rage   and like your fear   your anger   strength   knows – who</small>

11 Who knoweth the power of thine anger? even according to thy fear, so is thy wrath.

לִמְנוֹת יָמֵינוּ כֵּן הוֹדַע וְנָבִא לְבַב חָכְמָה:

<small>wisdom   heart   and we come   make us know   thus   our days   to assign</small>

12 So teach us to number our days, that we may apply our hearts unto wisdom.

שׁוּבָה יְהֹוָה עַד־מָתָי וְהִנָּחֵם עַל־עֲבָדֶיךָ:

<small>your servants - upon   and comfort them   when – until   ihvh   return</small>

13 Return, O LORD, how long? and let it repent thee concerning thy servants.

שַׂבְּעֵנוּ בַבֹּקֶר חַסְדֶּךָ וּנְרַנְּנָה וְנִשְׂמְחָה בְּכָל־יָמֵינוּ:

<small>our days – in all   and we be happy   and we shout w/ joy   your mercy   in morning   satisfy us</small>

14 O satisfy us early with thy mercy; that we may rejoice and be glad all our days.

שַׂמְּחֵנוּ כִּימוֹת עִנִּיתָנוּ שְׁנוֹת רָאִינוּ רָעָה:

<small>evil   we saw   years   you afflicted us   like days   make happy us</small>

15 Make us glad according to the days wherein thou hast afflicted us, and the years wherein we have seen evil.

יֵרָאֶה אֶל־עֲבָדֶיךָ פָעֳלֶךָ וַהֲדָרְךָ עַל־בְּנֵיהֶם:

| will see | your servants – unto | your works | and your majesty | their sons – upon |
|---|---|---|---|---|

16 Let thy work appear unto thy servants, and thy glory unto their children.

וִיהִי נֹעַם אֲדֹנָי אֱלֹהֵינוּ עָלֵינוּ

| and let | pleasantness | Adonai | our Elohim | upon us |
|---|---|---|---|---|

וּמַעֲשֵׂה יָדֵינוּ כּוֹנְנָה עָלֵינוּ

| and deeds | our hands | establish | upon us |
|---|---|---|---|

וּמַעֲשֵׂה יָדֵינוּ כּוֹנְנֵהוּ:

| and deeds | our hands | establish it |
|---|---|---|

17 And let the beauty of the LORD our God be upon us: and establish thou
the work of our hands upon us; yea, the work of our hands establish thou it.

# PSALM 105

ספר תהילים פרק קה

הוֹדוּ לַיהֹוָה קִרְאוּ בִשְׁמוֹ הוֹדִיעוּ בָעַמִּים עֲלִילוֹתָיו:

| his deeds | in people | you make known | in his name | you call | to ihvh | you thank |

1. O give thanks to the Lord; call upon his name; make known his deeds among the people.

שִׁירוּ לוֹ זַמְּרוּ־לוֹ שִׂיחוּ בְּכָל־נִפְלְאוֹתָיו:

| his mystical works – in all | you meditate | to him – you sing psalms | to him | you sing |

2. Sing to him, sing psalms to him; talk you of all his wondrous works.

הִתְהַלְלוּ בְּשֵׁם קָדְשׁוֹ יִשְׂמַח לֵב מְבַקְשֵׁי יְהֹוָה:

| ihvh | seekers | heart | he glad | his holiness | in name | you praise |

3. Glory in his holy name; let the heart of those who seek the Lord rejoice.

דִּרְשׁוּ יְהֹוָה וְעֻזּוֹ בַּקְּשׁוּ פָנָיו תָּמִיד:

| continually | his faces | you seek | and his strength | ihvh | you seek |

4. Seek the Lord, and his strength; seek his face continually.

זִכְרוּ נִפְלְאוֹתָיו אֲשֶׁר עָשָׂה מֹפְתָיו וּמִשְׁפְּטֵי־פִיו:

| his mouth - and judgments | his wonders | he does | which | his mystical works | you remember |

5. Remember his marvelous works that he has done; his wonders, and the judgments of his mouth;

זֶרַע אַבְרָהָם עַבְדּוֹ בְּנֵי יַעֲקֹב בְּחִירָיו:

| his chosen ones | Jacob | sons | his servant | Abraham | seed |

6. O seed of Abraham, his servant! O children of Jacob, his chosen!

הוּא יְהֹוָה אֱלֹהֵינוּ בְּכָל־הָאָרֶץ מִשְׁפָּטָיו:

| his judgments | the earth - in all | our Elohim | ihvh | he |

7. He is the Lord our God; his judgments are over all the earth.

זָכַר לְעוֹלָם בְּרִיתוֹ דָּבָר צִוָּה לְאֶלֶף דּוֹר:

| generation | to thousand | he commanded | speak | his covenant | forever | he remembered |

8. He has remembered his covenant for ever, the word which he commanded to a thousand generations.

אֲשֶׁר כָּרַת אֶת־אַבְרָהָם וּשְׁבוּעָתוֹ לְיִשְׂחָק:

| to Isaac | and his oath | Abraham - that | he cut | which |

9. The covenant which he made with Abraham, and his oath to Isaac;

וַיַּעֲמִידֶהָ לְיַעֲקֹב לְחֹק לְיִשְׂרָאֵל בְּרִית עוֹלָם:

| forever | covenant | to Israel | to statute | to Jacob | and he made it stand |

10. And confirmed the same to Jacob for a law, and to Israel for an everlasting covenant;

לְאמֹר לְךָ אֶתֵּן אֶת־אֶרֶץ כְּנַעַן חֶבֶל נַחֲלַתְכֶם:

| your inheritance | allotment | Canaan | land - that | I give | to you | saying |

11. Saying, To you I will give the land of Canaan, the lot of your inheritance;

בִּהְיוֹתָם מְתֵי מִסְפָּר כִּמְעַט וְגָרִים בָּהּ:

| in it | and sojourners | like little | number | few | in their being |

12. When they were but a few men in number; of little account and sojourners there.

וַיִּתְהַלְכוּ מִגּוֹי אֶל־גּוֹי מִמַּמְלָכָה אֶל־עַם אַחֵר:

| other | people -unto | from kingdom | nation – unto | from nations | and they walked |

13. When they went from one nation to another, from one kingdom to another people;

לֹא־הִנִּיחַ אָדָם לְעָשְׁקָם וַיּוֹכַח עֲלֵיהֶם מְלָכִים:

| kings | upon them | and he rebuked | to extort them | Adam | allowed - not |

14. He did not allow any man to do them wrong; he reproved kings for their sakes;

אַל־תִּגְּעוּ בִמְשִׁיחָי וְלִנְבִיאַי אַל־תָּרֵעוּ:

| you do evil – don't | and to my prophets | in my anointed ones | you touch – don't |

15. Saying, Do not touch my anointed, and do not do any harm to my prophets.

וַיִּקְרָא רָעָב עַל־הָאָרֶץ כָּל־מַטֵּה־לֶחֶם שָׁבָר:

| he broke | bread - stock – all | the earth –upon | famine | and he called |

16. Moreover he called for a famine upon the land; he broke every staff of bread.

שָׁלַח לִפְנֵיהֶם אִישׁ לְעֶבֶד נִמְכַּר יוֹסֵף:

| Joseph | he was sold | to servant | man | before them | he sent |

17. He sent a man before them, Joseph, who was sold as a slave;

עִנּוּ בַכֶּבֶל רַגְלָיו [רַגְלוֹ] בַּרְזֶל בָּאָה נַפְשׁוֹ:

| his soul | came | iron | his foot | in fetter | they afflicted |

18. (K) Whose foot they hurt with fetters; he was laid in iron;

עַד־עֵת בֹּא־דְבָרוֹ אִמְרַת יְהֹוָה צְרָפָתְהוּ:

| refined him | ihvh | word | his word – coming | season - till |

19. Until the time that his word came to pass; the word of the Lord had tested him.

שָׁלַח־מֶלֶךְ וַיַּתִּירֵהוּ מֹשֵׁל עַמִּים וַיְפַתְּחֵהוּ׃

and he opened him free   peoples   ruler   and he loosed him   king - sent

20. The king sent and released him; the ruler of the people let him go free.

שָׂמוֹ אָדוֹן לְבֵיתוֹ וּמֹשֵׁל בְּכָל־קִנְיָנוֹ׃

his possessions – in all   and ruler   to his house   master   set him

21. He made him lord of his house, and ruler of all his possessions;

לֶאְסֹר שָׂרָיו בְּנַפְשׁוֹ וּזְקֵנָיו יְחַכֵּם׃

he make wise them   and his old men   in his soul   his princes   to bind

22. To bind his princes at his pleasure; and teach his elders wisdom.

וַיָּבֹא יִשְׂרָאֵל מִצְרָיִם וְיַעֲקֹב גָּר בְּאֶרֶץ־חָם׃

Ham – in land   sojourned   and Jacob   Egypt   Israel   and he came

23. And Israel came into Egypt; and Jacob sojourned in the land of Ham.

וַיֶּפֶר אֶת־עַמּוֹ מְאֹד וַיַּעֲצִמֵהוּ מִצָּרָיו׃

from his adversaries   and he strengthened them   greatly   his people – that   and he made fruitful

24. And he increased his people greatly; and made them stronger than their enemies.

הָפַךְ לִבָּם לִשְׂנֹא עַמּוֹ לְהִתְנַכֵּל בַּעֲבָדָיו׃

in his servants   to act craftily   his people   to hate   their hearts   he turned

25. He turned their heart to hate his people, to deal craftily with his servants.

שָׁלַח מֹשֶׁה עַבְדּוֹ אַהֲרֹן אֲשֶׁר בָּחַר־בּוֹ׃

in him – he chose   which   Aaron   his servant   Moses   he sent

26. He sent Moses his servant; and Aaron whom he had chosen.

שָׂמוּ־בָם דִּבְרֵי אֹתוֹתָיו וּמֹפְתִים בְּאֶרֶץ חָם׃

Ham   in land   this wonders   his signs   speaking   in them - they placed

27. They performed his signs among them, and wonders in the land of Ham.

שָׁלַח חֹשֶׁךְ וַיַּחְשִׁךְ וְלֹא־מָרוּ אֶת־דְּבָרָיו [דְּבָרוֹ]׃

his speakings – that   they rebelled against – and not   it became dark   darkness   he sent

28. (K) He sent darkness, and made it dark; and they did not rebel against his word.

הָפַךְ אֶת־מֵימֵיהֶם לְדָם וַיָּמֶת אֶת־דְּגָתָם׃

their fish – that   and he made death   to blood   their waters – that   he turned

29. He turned their waters into blood, and caused their fish to die.

שָׁרַץ אַרְצָם צְפַרְדְּעִים בְּחַדְרֵי מַלְכֵיהֶם׃

their kings   in chambers   frogs   their land   swarmed

30. Their land swarmed with frogs, in the chambers of their kings.

אָמַר וַיָּבֹא עָרֹב כִּנִּים בְּכָל־גְּבוּלָם:

their borders – in all    lice    swarming flies    and it came    he said

31. He spoke, and there came swarms of flies and gnats in all their borders.

נָתַן גִּשְׁמֵיהֶם בָּרָד אֵשׁ לֶהָבוֹת בְּאַרְצָם:

in their land    blazing    fire    hail    their showers    he gave

32. He gave them hail for rain, and flaming fire in their land.

וַיַּךְ גַּפְנָם וּתְאֵנָתָם וַיְשַׁבֵּר עֵץ גְּבוּלָם:

their border    trees    and he broke    and their fig trees    their vines    and he smote

33. He struck their vines also and their fig trees; and broke the trees of their country.

אָמַר וַיָּבֹא אַרְבֶּה וְיֶלֶק וְאֵין מִסְפָּר:

number    and isn't    and hopping locusts    locust    and it came    he said

34. He spoke, and the swarming locusts came, and the hopping locusts without number.

וַיֹּאכַל כָּל־עֵשֶׂב בְּאַרְצָם וַיֹּאכַל פְּרִי אַדְמָתָם:

their ground    fruit    and it ate    in their land    plants – all    and they ate

35. And they ate up all the plants in their land, and devoured the fruit of their ground.

וַיַּךְ כָּל־בְּכוֹר בְּאַרְצָם רֵאשִׁית לְכָל־אוֹנָם:

their strength – to all    first ones    in their land    first born – all    and he smote

36. And he struck all the firstborn in their land, the first issue of all their strength.

וַיּוֹצִיאֵם בְּכֶסֶף וְזָהָב וְאֵין בִּשְׁבָטָיו כּוֹשֵׁל:

stumbling    in their tribes    and isn't    and gold    in silver    and he brought out them

37. And he brought them out with silver and gold; and among their tribes there was no one who stumbled.

שָׂמַח מִצְרַיִם בְּצֵאתָם כִּי־נָפַל פַּחְדָּם עֲלֵיהֶם:

upon them    their fear    fell – like    in their going out    Egypt    was happy

38. Egypt was glad when they departed; for the fear of them had fallen upon them.

פָּרַשׂ עָנָן לְמָסָךְ וְאֵשׁ לְהָאִיר לָיְלָה:

night    to the light    and fire    to cover    cloud    he spread

39. He spread a cloud for a covering; and fire to give light in the night.

שָׁאַל וַיָּבֵא שְׂלָו וְלֶחֶם שָׁמַיִם יַשְׂבִּיעֵם:

it satisfy them    heaven    and bread    quails    and he brought    asked

40. They asked, and he brought quails, and satisfied them with bread from heaven.

פָּתַח צוּר וַיָּזוּבוּ מָיִם הָלְכוּ בַּצִּיּוֹת נָהָר׃

| he opened | rock | and they gushed out | waters | it went | in dry places | river |

41. He opened the rock, and the waters gushed out; it ran in the dry places like
a river.

כִּי־זָכַר אֶת־דְּבַר קָדְשׁוֹ אֶת־אַבְרָהָם עַבְדּוֹ׃

| he remembered - like | speak – that | his holiness | Abraham – that | his servant |

42. For he remembered his holy promise, and Abraham his servant.

וַיּוֹצֵא עַמּוֹ בְשָׂשׂוֹן בְּרִנָּה אֶת־בְּחִירָיו׃

| and he brought out | his people | in elation | in joy shouting | his chosen ones – that |

43. And he brought out his people with joy, and his chosen with gladness;

וַיִּתֵּן לָהֶם אַרְצוֹת גּוֹיִם וַעֲמַל לְאֻמִּים יִירָשׁוּ׃

| and he gave | to them | lands | nations | and labor | to peoples | they seized |

44. And he gave them the lands of the nations; and they seized the labor of
the people,

בַּעֲבוּר יִשְׁמְרוּ חֻקָּיו וְתוֹרֹתָיו יִנְצֹרוּ הַלְלוּיָהּ׃

| in sake of | they heed | his statues | and his torahs | they preserve | praise yah |

45. That they might observe his statutes, and keep his Torot. Hallelujah! Lord.

# PSALM 137

ספר תהילים פרק קלז

עַל־נַהֲרוֹת בָּבֶל שָׁם יָשַׁבְנוּ
<br>we sat · there · in Babylon · rivers - upon

גַּם־בָּכִינוּ בְּזָכְרֵנוּ אֶת־צִיּוֹן:
<br>Zion - that · in we remembered · we wept - also

1. By the rivers of Babylon, there we sat down, we also wept, when we remembered Zion.

עַל־עֲרָבִים בְּתוֹכָהּ תָּלִינוּ כִּנֹּרוֹתֵינוּ:
<br>our lyres · we hung · in midst · the willows - upon

2. We hung our lyres on the willows in its midst.

כִּי שָׁם שְׁאֵלוּנוּ שׁוֹבֵינוּ דִּבְרֵי־שִׁיר
<br>song – words · our captors · asked us · there · like

וְתוֹלָלֵינוּ שִׂמְחָה שִׁירוּ לָנוּ מִשִּׁיר צִיּוֹן:
<br>Zion · from song · to us · you sing · happy · and our tormentors

3. For there those who carried us away captive required of us a song; and those who tormented us required of us mirth, saying, Sing us one of the songs of Zion.

אֵיךְ נָשִׁיר אֶת־שִׁיר יְהוָה עַל אַדְמַת נֵכָר:
<br>foreign · grounds · upon · ihvh · song – that · we sing · how

4. How shall we sing the Lord's song in a foreign land?

אִם־אֶשְׁכָּחֵךְ יְרוּשָׁלָםִ תִּשְׁכַּח יְמִינִי:
<br>my right hand · it forget · Jerusalem · I forget you - if

5. If I forget you, O Jerusalem, let my right hand forget her cunning.

תִּדְבַּק־לְשׁוֹנִי לְחִכִּי אִם־לֹא אֶזְכְּרֵכִי
<br>I remember you · not - if · to my palate · my tongue - it cling

אִם־לֹא אַעֲלֶה אֶת־יְרוּשָׁלַםִ עַל רֹאשׁ שִׂמְחָתִי:
<br>my happiness · head · upon · Jerusalem – that · I elevate · not - if

6. If I do not remember you, let my tongue cleave to the roof of my mouth; if I do not set Jerusalem above my highest joy.

זְכֹר יְהוָה לִבְנֵי אֱדוֹם אֵת יוֹם יְרוּשָׁלָםִ
<br>Jerusalem · day · that · Edomites · to sons · ihvh · remember

הָאֹמְרִים עָרוּ עָרוּ עַד הַיְסוֹד בָּהּ:

in it    the foundation    till    raze it    raze it    the saying ones

7. Remember, O Lord, against the Edomites, the day of Jerusalem; who said,
Raze it, raze it, to its foundation.

בַּת־בָּבֶל הַשְּׁדוּדָה

the devistating one    Babylon - daughter

אַשְׁרֵי שֶׁיְשַׁלֶּם־לָךְ אֶת־גְּמוּלֵךְ שֶׁגָּמַלְתְּ לָנוּ:

to us   that you rewarded   your reward – that   to you – that will pay them   happy

8. O daughter of Babylon, you are to be destroyed! Happy shall he be, who
repays you for what you have done to us!

אַשְׁרֵי שֶׁיֹּאחֵז וְנִפֵּץ אֶת־עֹלָלַיִךְ אֶל־הַסָּלַע:

the rock crag – onto   your babes – that   and shatter   that he grab   happy

9. Happy shall he be, who takes your little ones and dashes them against the
rock.

# PSALM 150

ספר תהילים פרק קנ

הַלְלוּיָהּ
you praise Ya

הַלְלוּ־אֵל בְּקָדְשׁוֹ
in his holy place    El - you praise

הַלְלוּהוּ בִּרְקִיעַ עֻזּוֹ׃
his power  in firmament  you praise him

1. Hallelujah! Praise God in his sanctuary! Praise him in the firmament of his power!

הַלְלוּהוּ בִגְבוּרֹתָיו
in his great acts    you praise him

הַלְלוּהוּ כְּרֹב גֻּדְלוֹ׃
his greatness  like much  praise him

2. Praise him for his mighty acts! Praise him according to his exceeding greatness!

הַלְלוּהוּ בְּתֵקַע שׁוֹפָר
shofar   in blast   you praise him

הַלְלוּהוּ בְּנֵבֶל וְכִנּוֹר׃
and harp  in lyre  you praise him

3. Praise him with the sound of the shofar! Praise him with the harp and the lyre!

הַלְלוּהוּ בְתֹף וּמָחוֹל
and dance  in tambourine  you praise him

הַלְלוּהוּ בְּמִנִּים וְעוּגָב׃
and reed pipes  in strings  praise him

4. Praise him with the tambourine and dance! Praise him with stringed instruments and the pipe!

הַלְלוּהוּ בְצִלְצְלֵי־שָׁמַע
hearing - in ringing  praise him

הַלְלוּהוּ בְּצִלְצְלֵי תְרוּעָה׃
alarm  in ringing  praise him

5. Praise him with sounding cymbals! Praise him with loud clashing cymbals!

כֹּל הַנְּשָׁמָה תְּהַלֵּל יָהּ

all   the (high) soul   it will praise   Ya

הַלְלוּיָהּ:

Ya   you praise

6. Let every thing that breathes praise the Lord! Hallelujah!

# PSALM 119

א

אַשְׁרֵי תְמִימֵי דָרֶךְ הַהֹלְכִים בְּתוֹרַת יְהֹוָה׃

| happy ones | perfect ones | way | the walking ones | in Torah | ihvh | 1 |

אַשְׁרֵי נֹצְרֵי עֵדֹתָיו בְּכָל־לֵב יִדְרְשׁוּהוּ׃

| happy ones | preserving ones | his testimonies | - in all | heart | they seek him | 2 |

אַף לֹא פָעֲלוּ עַוְלָה בִּדְרָכָיו הָלָכוּ׃

| then | not | they act | inequity | in his way | they walk | 3 |

אַתָּה צִוִּיתָה פִקֻּדֶיךָ לִשְׁמֹר מְאֹד׃

| you | commanded | your precepts | to heed | very | 4 |

אַחֲלַי יִכֹּנוּ דְרָכָי לִשְׁמֹר חֻקֶּיךָ׃

| oh me | they establish | my way | to heed | your statutes | 5 |

אָז לֹא אֵבוֹשׁ בְּהַבִּיטִי אֶל כָּל מִצְוֹתֶיךָ׃

| thus | not | I ashamed | in my observing | unto | all | your commandments | 6 |

אוֹדְךָ בְּיֹשֶׁר לֵבָב בְּלָמְדִי מִשְׁפְּטֵי צִדְקֶךָ׃

| I acclaim you | in upright | heart | in my learning | judgments | your righteousness | 7 |

אֶת חֻקֶּיךָ אֶשְׁמֹר אַל תַּעַזְבֵנִי עַד מְאֹד׃

| that | your statutes | I heed | don't | you forsake me | till | very | 8 |

## ב

9 בַּמֶּה יְזַכֶּה נַּעַר אֶת אָרְחוֹ לִשְׁמֹר כִּדְבָרֶךָ׃

like your speaking · to heed · his road · that · youth · purify · in what

10 בְּכָל לִבִּי דְרַשְׁתִּיךָ אַל תַּשְׁגֵּנִי מִמִּצְוֺתֶיךָ׃

from your commandments · you err me · don't · I sought you · my heart · in all

11 בְּלִבִּי צָפַנְתִּי אִמְרָתֶךָ לְמַעַן לֹא אֶחֱטָא לָךְ׃

to you · I sin · not · to end · your word · I secluded · in my heart

12 בָּרוּךְ אַתָּה יְהוָה לַמְּדֵנִי חֻקֶּיךָ׃

your statutes · teach me · ihvh · you · bless

13 בִּשְׂפָתַי סִפַּרְתִּי כֹּל מִשְׁפְּטֵי פִיךָ׃

your mouth · judgments · all · I recount · in my lips

14 בְּדֶרֶךְ עֵדְוֺתֶיךָ שַׂשְׂתִּי כְּעַל כָּל הוֹן׃

wealth · all · like upon · I rejoice · your testimonies · in way

15 בְּפִקֻּדֶיךָ אָשִׂיחָה וְאַבִּיטָה אֹרְחֹתֶיךָ׃

your roads · light · and I look intently · I meditate · in your precepts

16 בְּחֻקֹּתֶיךָ אֶשְׁתַּעֲשָׁע לֹא אֶשְׁכַּח דְּבָרֶךָ׃

your speaking · I forget · not · I revel · in your statutes

ג

גְּמֹל עַל עַבְדְּךָ אֶחְיֶה וְאֶשְׁמְרָה דְבָרֶךָ:

your speaking　and I heed　I live　your servant　upon　reward 17

גַּל עֵינַי וְאַבִּיטָה נִפְלָאוֹת מִתּוֹרָתֶךָ:

from your Torah　mystical　and I perceive　my eyes　unveil 18

גֵּר אָנֹכִי בָאָרֶץ אַל תַּסְתֵּר מִמֶּנִּי מִצְוֹתֶיךָ:

your commandments　from me　conceal　don't　in earth　I am　stranger 19

גָּרְסָה נַפְשִׁי לְתַאֲבָה אֶל מִשְׁפָּטֶיךָ בְכָל עֵת:

time　in all　your judgments　unto　to longing　my soul　shattered 20

גָּעַרְתָּ זֵדִים אֲרוּרִים הַשֹּׁגִים מִמִּצְוֹתֶיךָ:

from your commandments　erring ones　cursed ones　arrogant ones　you rebuke 21

גַּל מֵעָלַי חֶרְפָּה וָבוּז כִּי עֵדֹתֶיךָ נָצָרְתִּי:

I kept　your testimonies　like　and contempt　insult　from upon me　roll 22

גַּם יָשְׁבוּ שָׂרִים בִּי נִדְבָּרוּ עַבְדְּךָ יָשִׂיחַ בְּחֻקֶּיךָ:

in your statutes　meditates　your servant　they speak　in me　chiefs　they sat　also 23

גַּם עֵדֹתֶיךָ שַׁעֲשֻׁעָי אַנְשֵׁי עֲצָתִי:

my counselors　men　my choice delicacy　your testimonies　also 24

ד

דָּבְקָה לֶעָפָר נַפְשִׁי חַיֵּנִי כִּדְבָרֶךָ:

clings   to dust   my soul   give me life   like your speaking   25

דְּרָכַי סִפַּרְתִּי וַתַּעֲנֵנִי לַמְּדֵנִי חֻקֶּיךָ:

my path   I recounted   and you answered me   teach me   your statutes   26

דֶּרֶךְ פִּקּוּדֶיךָ הֲבִינֵנִי וְאָשִׂיחָה בְּנִפְלְאוֹתֶיךָ:

path   your precepts   the my understandings   the my understandings   and I meditate   in your mystical things   27

דָּלְפָה נַפְשִׁי מִתּוּגָה קַיְּמֵנִי כִּדְבָרֶךָ:

weary   my soul   from affliction   raise me   like your speaking   28

דֶּרֶךְ שֶׁקֶר הָסֵר מִמֶּנִּי וְתוֹרָתְךָ חָנֵּנִי:

the path   lie   remove   from me   and your Torah   give me grace   29

דֶּרֶךְ אֱמוּנָה בָחָרְתִּי מִשְׁפָּטֶיךָ שִׁוִּיתִי:

the path   faithfulness   I chose   your judgments   laid before me   30

דָּבַקְתִּי בְעֵדְוֹתֶיךָ יְהֹוָה אַל תְּבִישֵׁנִי:

I cleave   in your testimonies   ihvh   don't   you shame me   31

דֶּרֶךְ מִצְוֹתֶיךָ אָרוּץ כִּי תַרְחִיב לִבִּי:

the path   your commandments   I run   like   it enlarges   my heart   32

ה

הוֹרֵנִי יְהֹוָה דֶּרֶךְ חֻקֶּיךָ וְאֶצְּרֶנָּה עֵקֶב:

end — and I keep — your statutes — the way — ihvh — direct me — 33

הֲבִינֵנִי וְאֶצְּרָה תוֹרָתֶךָ וְאֶשְׁמְרֶנָּה בְכָל לֵב:

heart — in all — and I to heed — your Torah — and I keep — the understanding me — 34

הַדְרִיכֵנִי בִּנְתִיב מִצְוֹתֶיךָ כִּי בוֹ חָפָצְתִּי:

I delight — in it — like — your commandments — in track — the direct me — 35

הַט לִבִּי אֶל עֵדְוֹתֶיךָ וְאַל אֶל בָּצַע:

unjust gain — unto — and don't — your testimonies — unto — my heart — stretch out — 36

הַעֲבֵר עֵינַי מֵרְאוֹת שָׁוְא בִּדְרָכֶךָ חַיֵּנִי:

give me life — in your path — vanity — from seeings — my eyes — the turn away — 37

הָקֵם לְעַבְדְּךָ אִמְרָתֶךָ אֲשֶׁר לְיִרְאָתֶךָ:

to your fearing — which — your word — to your servant — confirm — 38

הַעֲבֵר חֶרְפָּתִי אֲשֶׁר יָגֹרְתִּי כִּי מִשְׁפָּטֶיךָ טוֹבִים:

good ones — your judgments — like — I shrink — which — my insult — the pass — 39

הִנֵּה תָּאַבְתִּי לְפִקֻּדֶיךָ בְּצִדְקָתְךָ חַיֵּנִי:

give me life — in your righteousness — to your precepts — my longing — here — 40

ו

וִיבֹאֻנִי    חֲסָדֶךָ   יְהֹוָה   תְּשׁוּעָתְךָ   כְּאִמְרָתֶךָ:
like your word    your salvation    ihvh    your mercies   and it comes to me 41

וְאֶעֱנֶה   חֹרְפִי   דָבָר   כִּי   בָטַחְתִּי   בִּדְבָרֶךָ:
in your speakings   my trust   like   speech   insults   and I answer 42

וְאַל   תַּצֵּל   מִפִּי   דְבַר   אֱמֶת   עַד   מְאֹד
very   till   truth   speech   from my mouth   you take away   and don't 43

כִּי   לְמִשְׁפָּטֶךָ   יִחָלְתִּי:
my hope   to your judgments   like

וְאֶשְׁמְרָה   תוֹרָתְךָ   תָמִיד   לְעוֹלָם   וָעֶד:
and ever   forever   continually   your Torah   and I heed 44

וְאֶתְהַלְּכָה   בָרְחָבָה   כִּי   פִקֻּדֶיךָ   דָרָשְׁתִּי:
my seeking   your precepts   like   in wideness   and I walk 45

וַאֲדַבְּרָה   בְעֵדֹתֶיךָ   נֶגֶד   מְלָכִים   וְלֹא   אֵבוֹשׁ:
I ashamed   and not   kings   in front   in your testimonies   and I speak 46

וְאֶשְׁתַּעֲשַׁע   בְּמִצְוֹתֶיךָ   אֲשֶׁר   אָהָבְתִּי:
I love   which   in your commandments   and I revel 47

וְאֶשָּׂא   כַפַּי   אֶל   מִצְוֹתֶיךָ   אֲשֶׁר   אָהָבְתִּי
I love   which   your commandments   unto   my palms   and I lift 48

וְאָשִׂיחָה   בְחֻקֶּיךָ:
in your statutes   and I meditate

ז

זְכֹר דָּבָר לְעַבְדֶּךָ עַל אֲשֶׁר יִחַלְתָּנִי׃

remember speak to your servant upon which it gives me hope 49

זֹאת נֶחָמָתִי בְעָנְיִי כִּי אִמְרָתְךָ חִיָּתְנִי׃

this my comfort in my affliction like your word gives me life 50

זֵדִים הֱלִיצֻנִי עַד מְאֹד מִתּוֹרָתְךָ לֹא נָטִיתִי׃

the arrogant taunts me till greatly from your Torah not I turned away 51

זָכַרְתִּי מִשְׁפָּטֶיךָ מֵעוֹלָם יְהוָה וָאֶתְנֶחָם׃

I remembered your judgments from ever ihvh and I comforted 52

זַלְעָפָה אֲחָזַתְנִי מֵרְשָׁעִים עֹזְבֵי תּוֹרָתֶךָ׃

sahara wind seized me from wicked ones forsaking ones your Torah 53

זְמִרוֹת הָיוּ לִי חֻקֶּיךָ בְּבֵית מְגוּרָי׃

singing psalms they were to me your statutes in house my sojourning 54

זָכַרְתִּי בַלַּיְלָה שִׁמְךָ יְהוָה וָאֶשְׁמְרָה תּוֹרָתֶךָ׃

I remembered in night your name ihvh and I heed your Torah 55

זֹאת הָיְתָה לִי כִּי פִקֻּדֶיךָ נָצָרְתִּי׃

this was to me like your precepts I have kept 56

ח

חֶלְקִי יְהוָֹה אָמַרְתִּי לִשְׁמֹר דְּבָרֶיךָ:
your speakings    to heed    I said    ihvh    my portion 57

חִלִּיתִי פָנֶיךָ בְכָל־לֵב חָנֵּנִי כְּאִמְרָתֶךָ:
like your word   give me grace   heart - in all   your face   I entreated 58

חִשַּׁבְתִּי דְרָכָי וָאָשִׁיבָה רַגְלַי אֶל עֵדֹתֶיךָ:
your testimonies   unto   my feet   and I returned   my ways   I considered 59

חַשְׁתִּי וְלֹא הִתְמַהְמָהְתִּי לִשְׁמֹר מִצְוֺתֶיךָ:
your commandments   to heed   I caused delay   and not   I hastened 60

חֶבְלֵי רְשָׁעִים עִוְּדֻנִי תּוֹרָתְךָ לֹא שָׁכָחְתִּי:
I forget   not   your Torah   roped me   wicked ones   bands 61

חֲצוֹת־לַיְלָה אָקוּם לְהוֹדוֹת לָךְ עַל
upon   to you   to acclaim   I rise   night - mid 62

מִשְׁפְּטֵי צִדְקֶךָ:
your righteous   judgments

חָבֵר אָנִי לְכָל־אֲשֶׁר יְרֵאוּךָ
they fear you   which - to all   I   companion 63

וּלְשֹׁמְרֵי פִּקּוּדֶיךָ:
your precepts   and to heeders

חַסְדְּךָ יְהוָֹה מָלְאָה הָאָרֶץ חֻקֶּיךָ לַמְּדֵנִי:
teach me   your statutes   the earth   fills   ihvh   your mercy 64

ט

טוֹב עָשִׂיתָ עִם־עַבְדְּךָ יְהֹוָה כִּדְבָרֶךָ׃

good | you did | your servant - with | ihvh | like your speaking   65

טוֹב טַעַם וָדַעַת לַמְּדֵנִי כִּי בְמִצְוֹתֶיךָ הֶאֱמָנְתִּי׃

good | discretion | and knowledge | teach me | like | in your commandments | I believe   66

טֶרֶם אֶעֱנֶה אֲנִי שֹׁגֵג וְעַתָּה אִמְרָתְךָ שָׁמָרְתִּי׃

before | I afflicted | I | erring | and now | your word | my heeding   67

טוֹב־אַתָּה וּמֵטִיב לַמְּדֵנִי חֻקֶּיךָ׃

you - good | and beneficial | teach me | your statutes   68

טָפְלוּ עָלַי שֶׁקֶר זֵדִים

they smear | upon me | lie | arrogant ones   69

אֲנִי בְּכָל־לֵב אֶצֹּר פִּקּוּדֶיךָ׃

I | heart - in all | I keep | your precepts

טָפַשׁ כַּחֵלֶב לִבָּם אֲנִי תּוֹרָתְךָ שִׁעֲשָׁעְתִּי׃

indigestible | like fat | their hearts | I | your Torah | my passion   70

טוֹב־לִי כִּי־עֻנֵּיתִי לְמַעַן אֶלְמַד חֻקֶּיךָ׃

to me - good | I afflicted - like | to end | I learn | your statutes   71

טוֹב־לִי תוֹרַת פִּיךָ מֵאַלְפֵי זָהָב וָכָסֶף׃

to me - good | Torah | your mouth | from thousands | gold | and silver   72

י

יָדֶיךָ עָשׂוּנִי וַיְכוֹנְנוּנִי הֲבִינֵנִי
the my understanding   and they establish me   they made me   your hands 73

וְאֶלְמְדָה מִצְוֹתֶיךָ:
your commandments   and I learn

יְרֵאֶיךָ יִרְאוּנִי וְיִשְׂמָחוּ כִּי לִדְבָרְךָ יִחָלְתִּי׃
I hoped   to your speakings   like   and they be happy   they see me   your fearing ones 74

יָדַעְתִּי יְהֹוָה כִּי־צֶדֶק מִשְׁפָּטֶיךָ וֶאֱמוּנָה עִנִּיתָנִי׃
afflicted me   and faithfulness   your judgments   righteous - like   ihvh   I know 75

יְהִי־נָא חַסְדְּךָ לְנַחֲמֵנִי כְּאִמְרָתְךָ לְעַבְדֶּךָ:
to your servant   like your word   to comfort me   your mercy   now - it is 76

יְבֹאוּנִי רַחֲמֶיךָ וְאֶחְיֶה כִּי תוֹרָתְךָ שַׁעֲשֻׁעָי׃
my delight   your Torah   like   and I live   your mercies   they come to me 77

יֵבֹשׁוּ זֵדִים כִּי־שֶׁקֶר עִוְּתוּנִי
dealt perversely to me   lie – like   arrogant ones   they ashamed 78

אֲנִי אָשִׂיחַ בְּפִקּוּדֶיךָ:
in your precepts   I meditate   I

יָשׁוּבוּ־לִי יְרֵאֶיךָ וְיֹדְעֵו עֵדֹתֶיךָ:
your testimonies   and they know   your fearing ones   to me - they return 79

יְהִי־לִבִּי תָמִים בְּחֻקֶּיךָ לְמַעַן לֹא אֵבוֹשׁ:
I be ashamed   not   to end   in your statutes   perfect   my heart – will be 80

כ

כָּלְתָה לִתְשׁוּעָתְךָ נַפְשִׁי לִדְבָרְךָ יִחָלְתִּי׃

| my hope | to your speakings | my soul | to your salvation | languishes | 81 |

כָּלוּ עֵינַי לְאִמְרָתֶךָ לֵאמֹר מָתַי תְּנַחֲמֵנִי׃

| you comfort me | when | to say | to your word | my eyes | they fail | 82 |

כִּי־הָיִיתִי כְּנֹאד בְּקִיטוֹר חֻקֶּיךָ לֹא שָׁכָחְתִּי׃

| I forget | not | your statutes | in smoke | like skin bottle | I was - like | 83 |

כַּמָּה יְמֵי עַבְדֶּךָ מָתַי תַּעֲשֶׂה בְרֹדְפַי מִשְׁפָּט׃

| judgment | in my persecution | you do | when | your servant | days | how many | 84 |

כָּרוּ־לִי זֵדִים שִׁיחוֹת אֲשֶׁר לֹא כְתוֹרָתֶךָ׃

| like your Torah | not | which | pits | proud ones | to me - they dig | 85 |

כָּל־מִצְוֹתֶיךָ אֱמוּנָה שֶׁקֶר רְדָפוּנִי עָזְרֵנִי׃

| help me | they persecute me | lie | faithful | your commandments - all | 86 |

כִּמְעַט כִּלּוּנִי בָאָרֶץ וַאֲנִי לֹא עָזַבְתִּי פִּקּוּדֶיךָ׃

| your precepts | forsaken | not | and I | in earth | finished me | like little | 87 |

כְּחַסְדְּךָ חַיֵּנִי וְאֶשְׁמְרָה עֵדוּת פִּיךָ׃

| your mouth | testimonies | and I heed | give me life | your mercy | like | 88 |

## ל

לְעוֹלָם יְהֹוָה דְּבָרְךָ נִצָּב בַּשָּׁמָיִם:

in heavens   fixed   your speakings   ihvh   to forever 89

לְדֹר וָדֹר אֱמוּנָתֶךָ כּוֹנַנְתָּ אֶרֶץ וַתַּעֲמֹד:

and it stands   earth   established   your faithfulness   and generation   to generation 90

לְמִשְׁפָּטֶיךָ עָמְדוּ הַיּוֹם כִּי הַכֹּל עֲבָדֶיךָ:

your servants   the all   like   the day   they stand   to your judgments 91

לוּלֵי תוֹרָתְךָ שַׁעֲשֻׁעָי אָז אָבַדְתִּי בְעָנְיִי:

in my affliction   I perished   then   my delight   your Torah   unless 92

לְעוֹלָם לֹא אֶשְׁכַּח פִּקּוּדֶיךָ כִּי בָם חִיִּיתָנִי:

give life to me   in them   like   your precepts   I forget   not   to forever 93

לְךָ אֲנִי הוֹשִׁיעֵנִי כִּי פִקּוּדֶיךָ דָרָשְׁתִּי:

I sought   your precepts   like   save me   I   to you 94

לִי קִוּוּ רְשָׁעִים לְאַבְּדֵנִי עֵדֹתֶיךָ אֶתְבּוֹנָן:

I understand   your testimonies   to destroy me   the wicked   they stretched to   to me 95

לְכָל תִּכְלָה רָאִיתִי קֵץ רְחָבָה מִצְוָתְךָ מְאֹד:

very   your commandment   broad   end   I have seen   perfection   to all 96

מ

מָה אָהַבְתִּי תוֹרָתֶךָ כָּל הַיּוֹם הִיא שִׂיחָתִי׃

97 what | I love | your Torah | all | the day | it | my meditation

מֵאֹיְבַי תְּחַכְּמֵנִי מִצְוֹתֶךָ כִּי לְעוֹלָם הִיא לִי׃

98 from my enemies | It makes me wise | your commandments | like | to forever | it | to me

מִכָּל מְלַמְּדַי הִשְׂכַּלְתִּי כִּי עֵדְוֹתֶיךָ שִׂיחָה לִי׃

99 from all | my teachers | caused me to be wise | like | your testimonies | meditation | to me

מִזְּקֵנִים אֶתְבּוֹנָן כִּי פִקּוּדֶיךָ נָצָרְתִּי׃

100 from old ones | I understand | like | your precepts | I keep

מִכָּל אֹרַח רָע כָּלִאתִי רַגְלָי

101 from all | road | bad | I refrained | my feet

לְמַעַן אֶשְׁמֹר דְּבָרֶךָ׃

102 to end | I heed | your speaking

מִמִּשְׁפָּטֶיךָ לֹא סָרְתִּי כִּי אַתָּה הוֹרֵתָנִי׃

102 from your judgments | not | I departed | like | you | direct me

מַה נִּמְלְצוּ לְחִכִּי אִמְרָתֶךָ מִדְּבַשׁ לְפִי׃

103 what | they sweet | to my palate | your word | from honey | to my mouth

מִפִּקּוּדֶיךָ אֶתְבּוֹנָן

104 from your precepts | I understand

עַל כֵּן שָׂנֵאתִי כָּל אֹרַח שָׁקֶר׃

lie | road | all | I hate | thus | upon

נ

נֵר לְרַגְלִי דְבָרֶךָ וְאוֹר לִנְתִיבָתִי:
to my tracks    and light    your speaking    to my feet    lamp 105

נִשְׁבַּעְתִּי וָאֲקַיֵּמָה לִשְׁמֹר מִשְׁפְּטֵי צִדְקֶךָ:
your righteous    judgments    to heed    and I confirm    I swore 106

נַעֲנֵיתִי עַד מְאֹד יְהֹוָה חַיֵּנִי כִדְבָרֶךָ:
like your speaking    give me life    ihvh    very    till    I am afflicted 107

נִדְבוֹת פִּי רְצֵה נָא יְהֹוָה וּמִשְׁפָּטֶיךָ לַמְּדֵנִי:
teach me    and your judgments    ihvh    now    accept    my mouth    offerings 108

נַפְשִׁי בְכַפִּי תָמִיד וְתוֹרָתְךָ לֹא שָׁכָחְתִּי:
I forget    not    and your Torah    always    in my palm    my soul 109

נָתְנוּ רְשָׁעִים פַּח לִי וּמִפִּקּוּדֶיךָ לֹא תָעִיתִי:
I error    not    and from your precepts    to me    snare    wicked ones    they give 110

נָחַלְתִּי עֵדְוֹתֶיךָ לְעוֹלָם כִּי שְׂשׂוֹן לִבִּי הֵמָּה:
they are    my heart    rejoicing    like    to forever    your testimonies    my heritage 111

נָטִיתִי לִבִּי לַעֲשׂוֹת חֻקֶּיךָ לְעוֹלָם עֵקֶב:
very end    to forever    your statutes    to doings    my heart    I stretched 112

ס

סְעַפִים שָׂנֵאתִי וְתוֹרָתְךָ אָהָבְתִּי:
I love    and your Torah    I hate    plotting evil  113

סִתְרִי    וּמָגִנִּי אַתָּה לִדְבָרְךָ יִחָלְתִּי:
I hoped    to your speaking    you    and my shield    my concealment  114

סוּרוּ מִמֶּנִּי מְרֵעִים וְאֶצְּרָה מִצְוֺת    אֱלֹהָי:
my Elohim    commandments    I keep    from evil ones    from me    depart  115

סָמְכֵנִי כְאִמְרָתְךָ וְאֶחְיֶה וְאַל תְּבִישֵׁנִי מִשִּׂבְרִי:
from my hope    you ashame me    and don't    and I live    like your word    support me  116

סְעָדֵנִי וְאִוָּשֵׁעָה וְאֶשְׁעָה בְחֻקֶּיךָ תָמִיד:
always    in your statutes    and I do    and I be saved    sustain me  117

סָלִיתָ    כָּל שׁוֹגִים מֵחֻקֶּיךָ    כִּי שֶׁקֶר תַּרְמִיתָם:
their deceits    lie    like from your statutes    erring ones    all    you trampled  118

סִגִים הִשְׁבַּתָּ כָל רִשְׁעֵי אָרֶץ
earth    wicked ones    all    you purged    drosses  119

לָכֵן אָהַבְתִּי עֵדֹתֶיךָ:
your testimonies    I love    to thus

סָמַר מִפַּחְדְּךָ בְשָׂרִי וּמִמִּשְׁפָּטֶיךָ יָרֵאתִי:
I fear    and from your judgments    my flesh    from your awe    bristles  120

ע

עָשִׂיתִי מִשְׁפָּט וָצֶדֶק    בַּל תַּנִּיחֵנִי לְעֹשְׁקָי:

to my oppressors  you leave me  in not    and righteousness  judgment     I did 121

עֲרֹב עַבְדְּךָ לְטוֹב אַל יַעַשְׁקֻנִי זֵדִים:

arrogant ones  they oppress me  don't  to good  your servant  surety 122

עֵינַי כָּלוּ לִישׁוּעָתֶךָ וּלְאִמְרַת צִדְקֶךָ:

your righteousness  and to words  to your salvation  they fail  my eyes 123

עֲשֵׂה עִם עַבְדְּךָ כְחַסְדֶּךָ וְחֻקֶּיךָ לַמְּדֵנִי:

teach me  and your statutes  like your mercy  your servant  with    do 124

עַבְדְּךָ אָנִי הֲבִינֵנִי וְאֵדְעָה עֵדֹתֶיךָ:

your testimonies  and I know  the my understanding  I    your servant 125

עֵת לַעֲשׂוֹת לַיהוָה הֵפֵרוּ תּוֹרָתֶךָ:

your Torah  they voided  to ihvh    to doings  time 126

עַל כֵּן אָהַבְתִּי מִצְוֹתֶיךָ מִזָּהָב וּמִפָּז:

and from pure gold  from gold  your commandments  I love  thus  upon 127

עַל כֵּן כָּל פִּקּוּדֵי כֹל יִשָּׁרְתִּי

I upright  all  precepts  all  thus  upon 128

כָּל אֹרַח שֶׁקֶר שָׂנֵאתִי:

I hate  lie  road  all

פ

פְּלָאוֹת עֵדְוֺתֶיךָ עַל כֵּן נְצָרָתַם נַפְשִׁי׃
<br>my soul   keeping them   thus   upon   your testimonies   mystical ones   129

פֵּתַח דְּבָרֶיךָ יָאִיר מֵבִין פְּתָיִים׃
<br>simple ones   from understanding   it lights   your speaking   opening   130

פִּי פָּעַרְתִּי וָאֶשְׁאָפָה כִּי לְמִצְוֺתֶיךָ יָאָבְתִּי׃
<br>it I crave   to your commandments   like   and I pant   I gape   my mouth   131

פְּנֵה אֵלַי וְחָנֵּנִי כְּמִשְׁפָּט לְאֹהֲבֵי שְׁמֶךָ׃
<br>your name   to lovers   like judgment   and grace me   unto me   face   132

פְּעָמַי הָכֵן בְּאִמְרָתֶךָ וְאַל תַּשְׁלֶט בִּי כָל אָוֶן׃
<br>inequity   all   in me   it dominate   and don't   in your word   establish   my steps   133

פְּדֵנִי מֵעֹשֶׁק אָדָם וְאֶשְׁמְרָה פִּקּוּדֶיךָ׃
<br>your precepts   and I heed   Adam   from oppression   deliver me   134

פָּנֶיךָ הָאֵר בְּעַבְדֶּךָ וְלַמְּדֵנִי אֶת חֻקֶּיךָ׃
<br>your statutes   that   and teach me   in your servant   the light   your face   135

פַּלְגֵי מַיִם יָרְדוּ עֵינָי עַל לֹא שָׁמְרוּ תוֹרָתֶךָ׃
<br>your Torah   they heed   not   upon   my eyes   they descend   water   streams   136

צ

צַדִּיק אַתָּה יְהֹוָה וְיָשָׁר מִשְׁפָּטֶיךָ:
your judgments and upright ihvh you righteous 137

צִוִּיתָ צֶדֶק עֵדֹתֶיךָ וֶאֱמוּנָה מְאֹד:
very and faithfulness your testimonies righteousness you commanded 138

צִמְּתַתְנִי קִנְאָתִי כִּי שָׁכְחוּ דְבָרֶיךָ צָרָי:
my adversaries your speakings they forgot like my zeal wipes out me 139

צְרוּפָה אִמְרָתְךָ מְאֹד וְעַבְדְּךָ אֲהֵבָהּ:
loves it and your servant very your word permutated 140

צָעִיר אָנֹכִי וְנִבְזֶה פִּקֻּדֶיךָ לֹא שָׁכָחְתִּי:
I forget not your precepts and despised I am inferior 141

צִדְקָתְךָ צֶדֶק לְעוֹלָם וְתוֹרָתְךָ אֱמֶת:
truth and your Torah to forever righteousness your righteousness 142

צַר־וּמָצוֹק מְצָאוּנִי מִצְוֹתֶיךָ שַׁעֲשֻׁעָי:
my delight your commandments found me and anguish - trouble 143

צֶדֶק עֵדְוֹתֶיךָ לְעוֹלָם הֲבִינֵנִי וְאֶחְיֶה:
and I live the my understanding to forever your testimonies righteous 144

ק

קָרָאתִי בְכָל־לֵב עֲנֵנִי יְהוָֹה חֻקֶּיךָ אֶצֹּרָה׃

I keep   your statutes   ihvh   answer me   heart - in all   I called   145

קְרָאתִיךָ הוֹשִׁיעֵנִי וְאֶשְׁמְרָה עֵדֹתֶיךָ׃

your testimonies   I heed   save me   I call you   146

קִדַּמְתִּי בַנֶּשֶׁף וָאֲשַׁוֵּעָה לִדְבָרְיךָ יִחָלְתִּי׃

my hope   to your speakings   and I implore   in gloom   I precede   147

קִדְּמוּ עֵינַי אַשְׁמֻרוֹת לָשִׂיחַ בְּאִמְרָתֶךָ׃

in your word   to meditate   watches of night   my eyes   they precede   148

קוֹלִי שִׁמְעָה כְחַסְדֶּךָ יְהוָֹה כְּמִשְׁפָּטֶךָ חַיֵּנִי׃

give me life   like your judgment   ihvh   like your mercy   you hear   my voice   149

קָרְבוּ רֹדְפֵי זִמָּה מִתּוֹרָתְךָ רָחָקוּ׃

they far   from your Torah   mischief   pursuers   they near   150

קָרוֹב אַתָּה יְהוָֹה וְכָל־מִצְוֹתֶיךָ אֱמֶת׃

truth   your commandments - and all   ihvh   you   near   151

קֶדֶם יָדַעְתִּי מֵעֵדֹתֶיךָ כִּי לְעוֹלָם יְסַדְתָּם׃

you founded them   to forever   like   from your testimonies   I know   of ancient time   152

ר

רְאֵה־עָנְיִי וְחַלְּצֵנִי כִּי־תוֹרָתְךָ לֹא שָׁכָחְתִּי:
<small>I forget    not    your Torah – like   and liberate me   my affliction – see 153</small>

רִיבָה רִיבִי וּגְאָלֵנִי לְאִמְרָתְךָ חַיֵּנִי:
<small>give me life   to your word  and redeem me  my contention  contend 154</small>

רָחוֹק מֵרְשָׁעִים יְשׁוּעָה כִּי־חֻקֶּיךָ לֹא דָרָשׁוּ:
<small>they sought   not  your statutes - like  salvation  from wicked ones  far 155</small>

רַחֲמֶיךָ רַבִּים יְהוָֹה כְּמִשְׁפָּטֶיךָ חַיֵּנִי:
<small>give me life   like your judgments  ihvh  many ones  your compassion 156</small>

רַבִּים רֹדְפַי וְצָרָי מֵעֵדְוֹתֶיךָ
<small>from your testimonies  and my adversaries  my persecutors  many 157</small>

לֹא נָטִיתִי:
<small>I turned aside   not</small>

רָאִיתִי בֹגְדִים וָאֶתְקוֹטָטָה אֲשֶׁר אִמְרָתְךָ
<small>your word  which  and that I disgusted  in transgressor ones  I see 158</small>

לֹא שָׁמָרוּ:
<small>they heed   not</small>

רְאֵה כִּי־פִקּוּדֶיךָ אָהָבְתִּי יְהוָֹה כְּחַסְדְּךָ חַיֵּנִי:
<small>give me life  like your mercy  ihvh  I love  your precepts - like  I see 159</small>

רֹאשׁ־דְּבָרְךָ אֱמֶת וּלְעוֹלָם
<small>and to forever  truth  your speaking – beginning 160</small>

כָּל־מִשְׁפַּט צִדְקֶךָ:
<small>your righteousness  judgment - all</small>

שׁ

שָׂרִים רְדָפוּנִי חִנָּם וּמִדְּבָרֶיךָ פָּחַד לִבִּי:

| princes | persecute me | without cause | and from your speakings | awe | my heart |
|---|---|---|---|---|---|

161

שָׂשׂ אָנֹכִי עַל־אִמְרָתֶךָ כְּמוֹצֵא שָׁלָל רָב:

| rejoicing | I am | your word – upon | like finder | booty | much |
|---|---|---|---|---|---|

162

שֶׁקֶר שָׂנֵאתִי וַאֲתַעֵבָה תּוֹרָתְךָ אָהָבְתִּי:

| lie | I hate | and I loathe | your Torah | I love |
|---|---|---|---|---|

163

שֶׁבַע בַּיּוֹם הִלַּלְתִּיךָ עַל מִשְׁפְּטֵי צִדְקֶךָ:

| seven | in day | I praise you | upon | judgments | your righteousness |
|---|---|---|---|---|---|

164

שָׁלוֹם רָב לְאֹהֲבֵי תוֹרָתֶךָ וְאֵין לָמוֹ מִכְשׁוֹל:

| peace | much | to lovers | your Torah | and isn't | to them | stumbling block |
|---|---|---|---|---|---|---|

165

שִׂבַּרְתִּי לִישׁוּעָתְךָ יְהֹוָה וּמִצְוֹתֶיךָ עָשִׂיתִי:

| I hope | to your salvation | ihvh | and your commandments | I do |
|---|---|---|---|---|

166

שָׁמְרָה נַפְשִׁי עֵדֹתֶיךָ וָאֹהֲבֵם מְאֹד:

| heeds | my soul | your testimonies | and I love them | very |
|---|---|---|---|---|

167

שָׁמַרְתִּי פִקּוּדֶיךָ וְעֵדֹתֶיךָ

| I heed | your precepts | and your testimonies |
|---|---|---|

168

כִּי כָל־דְּרָכַי נֶגְדֶּךָ:

| like | my ways – all | in front of you |
|---|---|---|

ת

תִּקְרַב רִנָּתִי לְפָנֶיךָ יְהוָֹה כִּדְבָרְךָ הֲבִינֵנִי:

the my understanding   like your speaking   ihvh   to your face   my joyful shout   it near   169

תָּבוֹא תְּחִנָּתִי לְפָנֶיךָ כְּאִמְרָתְךָ הַצִּילֵנִי:

the rescue me   like your word   before you   my supplication   it come   170

תַּבַּעְנָה שְׂפָתַי תְּהִלָּה כִּי תְלַמְּדֵנִי חֻקֶּיךָ:

your statutes   you teach me   like   praise   my lips   utter   171

תַּעַן לְשׁוֹנִי אִמְרָתֶךָ כִּי כָל־מִצְוֹתֶיךָ צֶּדֶק:

right   your commandments - all   like   your word   my tongue   it answers   172

תְּהִי־יָדְךָ לְעָזְרֵנִי כִּי פִקּוּדֶיךָ בָחָרְתִּי:

I chose   your precepts   like   to help me   your hand - it be   173

תָּאַבְתִּי לִישׁוּעָתְךָ יְהוָֹה וְתוֹרָתְךָ שַׁעֲשֻׁעָי:

my delight   and your Torah   ihvh   to your salvation   I crave   174

תְּחִי־נַפְשִׁי וּתְהַלְלֶךָּ וּמִשְׁפָּטֶךָ יַעְזְרֻנִי:

they help me   and your judgments   and it praises you   my soul - it live   175

תָּעִיתִי כְּשֶׂה אֹבֵד בַּקֵּשׁ עַבְדֶּךָ

your servant   seek   lost   like sheep   I strayed   176

כִּי מִצְוֹתֶיךָ לֹא שָׁכָחְתִּי:

I forget   not   your commandments   like

## SUPPLICATION

It is very important that after you do your praying and meditations, you take the time to ask for what you want. The Baal Shem Tov, Rabbi Nachman, and many other great kabbalah teachers have stated that this as a very important stage. After saying prayers and doing the meditations, be sure and ask, with clarity, WHAT YOU WANT.

**APPENDIX**

## Rabbi Nachman:

Rabbi Nachman, ben Simcha AKA Rabbi Nachman of Breslov. also known as Reb Nachman of Bratslav, Reb Nachman Breslover, Nachman from Uman. He was born April 4, 1772 Medzhybizh, Ukraine, and died October 16, 1810, at the age of 38.

He believed in being close to God by speaking to God in normal conversation "as you would with a best friend." The concept of hitbodedut is central to his thinking.

He taught that his followers should spend an hour alone each day, talking aloud to God in his or her own words, as if "talking to a good friend." This is in addition to the prayers in the siddur. Breslover Hasidim still follow this practice today, which is known as hitbodedut (literally, "to make oneself be in solitude"). Rebbe Nachman taught that the best place to do hitbodedut was in a field or forest, among the natural works of God's creation.

## Baal Shem Tov, Rabbi Yisroel ben Elieze

The Baal Shem Tov (nickname "BeShT,") was the grandfather of Rabbi Nachman. He was the founder of the Hasidic movement. He was orphaned. born in what is today the Ukraine. according to chasidic tradition, he learned how to work miracles with the name of God. born on the 18th of Elul 5458 (August 27, 1698) to Rabbi Eliezer and his wife Sarah. The Baal Shem Tov passed away on Shavuos, 5520 (May 23, 1760) age 62, having founded the Chassidic movement that lives on today.

מאתיים שנה להסתלקות

׳בי ישראל בעל שם טוב

יוצר החסידות

חק״ך–תש״ך

BI-CENTENAIRE DE LA MORT DE
RABBI ISRAËL BAAL CHEM TOV
FONDATEUR DU HASSIDISME

## SHEMA

**DEUT 6:49-54**

ספר דברים פרק ו

שְׁמַע יִשְׂרָאֵל יְהֹוָה אֱלֹהֵינוּ יְהֹוָה אֶחָד:
one · ihvh · our God · ihvh · Israel · hear 49

[ברוך שם כבוד מלכותו לעולם ועד]

וְאָהַבְתָּ אֵת יְהֹוָה אֱלֹהֶיךָ
your God · ihvh · that · and love 50

בְּכָל־לְבָבְךָ וּבְכָל־נַפְשְׁךָ וּבְכָל־מְאֹדֶךָ:
your might - and in all · your soul - and in all · your heart - in all

וְהָיוּ הַדְּבָרִים הָאֵלֶּה
the these · the words · and it is 51

אֲשֶׁר אָנֹכִי מְצַוְּךָ הַיּוֹם עַל־לְבָבֶךָ:
your heart – upon · the day · commanding you · I · which

וְשִׁנַּנְתָּם לְבָנֶיךָ וְדִבַּרְתָּ בָּם בְּשִׁבְתְּךָ בְּבֵיתֶךָ
in your house · in your sitting · in them · and you speak · to your sons · and train them 52

וּבְלֶכְתְּךָ בַדֶּרֶךְ וּבְשָׁכְבְּךָ וּבְקוּמֶךָ:
and in your rising · and in your lying down · in path · and in your going

וּקְשַׁרְתָּם לְאוֹת עַל־יָדֶךָ
your hand – upon · to sign · and bind them 53

וְהָיוּ לְטֹטָפֹת בֵּין עֵינֶיךָ:
your eyes · between · frontlets · and they will be

וּכְתַבְתָּם עַל־מְזֻזוֹת בֵּיתֶךָ וּבִשְׁעָרֶיךָ:
and in your gates · your house · door mantles – upon · and write them 54

## DEUT 11:13-21

ספר דברים פרק יא

וְהָיָה אִם־שָׁמֹעַ תִּשְׁמְעוּ אֶל־מִצְוֹתַי
<small>my commandments – unto    you hear    hearing – with    and it be ۱۳</small>

אֲשֶׁר אָנֹכִי מְצַוֶּה אֶתְכֶם הַיּוֹם
<small>the day    to you    commanding    I am    which</small>

לְאַהֲבָה אֶת־יְהוָֹה אֱלֹהֵיכֶם
<small>your Elohim    ihvh – that    to love</small>

וּלְעָבְדוֹ בְּכָל־לְבַבְכֶם וּבְכָל־נַפְשְׁכֶם:
<small>your souls - and in all    your hearts - in all    and to his service</small>

וְנָתַתִּי מְטַר־אַרְצְכֶם בְּעִתּוֹ יוֹרֶה וּמַלְקוֹשׁ
<small>and latter rain    first rain    in season    your lands – rain    and I give ۱٤</small>

וְאָסַפְתָּ דְגָנֶךָ וְתִירֹשְׁךָ וְיִצְהָרֶךָ:
<small>and your oil    and your grape juice    your grain    and you gather</small>

וְנָתַתִּי עֵשֶׂב בְּשָׂדְךָ לִבְהֶמְתֶּךָ וְאָכַלְתָּ וְשָׂבָעְתָּ:
<small>and you full    and you eat    to your cattle    in your fields    grass    and I give ۱٥</small>

הִשָּׁמְרוּ לָכֶם פֶּן־יִפְתֶּה לְבַבְכֶם
<small>your hearts    allure – lest    to you    you cause to heed ۱٦</small>

וְסַרְתֶּם וַעֲבַדְתֶּם אֱלֹהִים אֲחֵרִים
<small>other ones    Elohim    and you serve    and you depart</small>

וְהִשְׁתַּחֲוִיתֶם לָהֶם:
<small>to them    and the bow them</small>

וְחָרָה אַף־יְהוָֹה בָּכֶם וְעָצַר אֶת־הַשָּׁמַיִם
<small>the heavens – that    and prevail    in you    ihvh – anger    and kindled ۱٧</small>

וְלֹא־יִהְיֶה מָטָר
<small>rain    there will be - and not</small>

וְהָאֲדָמָה לֹא תִתֵּן אֶת־יְבוּלָהּ
<small>produce - that    gives    not    and the soil</small>

וַאֲבַדְתֶּם מְהֵרָה מֵעַל הָאָרֶץ הַטֹּבָה

the good · the earth · from upon · quickly · and you serve

אֲשֶׁר יְהוָֹה נֹתֵן לָכֶם:

to you · gave · ihvh · which

וְשַׂמְתֶּם אֶת־דְּבָרַי אֵלֶּה

these · my speakings – that · and you put 18

עַל־לְבַבְכֶם וְעַל־נַפְשְׁכֶם

your souls - and upon · your hearts – upon

וּקְשַׁרְתֶּם אֹתָם לְאוֹת עַל־יֶדְכֶם

your hands - upon · to sign · to them · and you bind

וְהָיוּ לְטוֹטָפֹת בֵּין עֵינֵיכֶם:

your eyes · between · to frontlets · and they be

וְלִמַּדְתֶּם אֹתָם אֶת־בְּנֵיכֶם

your sons – that · to them · and you teach 19

לְדַבֵּר בָּם בְּשִׁבְתְּךָ בְּבֵיתֶךָ

in your house · in your sitting · to them · to speak

וּבְלֶכְתְּךָ בַדֶּרֶךְ וּבְשָׁכְבְּךָ וּבְקוּמֶךָ:

and in your rising · and in your lying down · in way · and in your going

וּכְתַבְתָּם עַל־מְזוּזוֹת בֵּיתֶךָ וּבִשְׁעָרֶיךָ:

and in your gates · your house · door posts – upon · and write them 20

לְמַעַן יִרְבּוּ יְמֵיכֶם וִימֵי בְּנֵיכֶם עַל הָאֲדָמָה

the ground · upon · your sons · and day · your days · they many · to end 21

אֲשֶׁר נִשְׁבַּע יְהוָֹה לַאֲבֹתֵיכֶם לָתֵת לָהֶם

to them · to give · to your fathers · ihvh · swore · which

כִּימֵי הַשָּׁמַיִם עַל־הָאָרֶץ:

the earth – upon · the heaven · like days

# NUMBERS 15:37-41

ספר במדבר פרק טו

וַיֹּאמֶר יְהֹוָה אֶל־מֹשֶׁה לֵּאמֹר׃
to say    Moses – unto    ihvh    and said 37

דַּבֵּר אֶל־בְּנֵי יִשְׂרָאֵל וְאָמַרְתָּ אֲלֵהֶם
unto them    and you say    Israel    sons – upon    speak 38

וְעָשׂוּ לָהֶם צִיצִת עַל־כַּנְפֵי בִגְדֵיהֶם לְדֹרֹתָם
to their generations   their garments   fringes – upon   tsitsit   to them   and you make

וְנָתְנוּ עַל־צִיצִת הַכָּנָף פְּתִיל תְּכֵלֶת׃
blue    border    the fringe    tsitsit - upon    and they give

וְהָיָה לָכֶם לְצִיצִת וּרְאִיתֶם אֹתוֹ
to it    and you see    to tsitsit    to you    and it be 39

וּזְכַרְתֶּם אֶת־כָּל־מִצְוֹת יְהֹוָה
ihvh    commandments - all - that    and you remember

וַעֲשִׂיתֶם אֹתָם וְלֹא תָתוּרוּ אַחֲרֵי לְבַבְכֶם
your hearts    after    you seek    and not    to them    and you do

וְאַחֲרֵי עֵינֵיכֶם אֲשֶׁר־אַתֶּם זֹנִים אַחֲרֵיהֶם׃
after them    adulterate    that you – which    your eyes    and after

לְמַעַן תִּזְכְּרוּ וַעֲשִׂיתֶם אֶת־כָּל־מִצְוֹתָי
my commandments – all – that   and you do   you remember   to end 40

וִהְיִיתֶם קְדֹשִׁים לֵאלֹהֵיכֶם׃
to your Elohim    holy ones    and you be

אֲנִי יְהֹוָה אֱלֹהֵיכֶם
your Elohim    ihvh    I 41

אֲשֶׁר הוֹצֵאתִי אֶתְכֶם מֵאֶרֶץ מִצְרַיִם
Egypt    from land    to you    I brought out    which

לִהְיוֹת לָכֶם לֵאלֹהִים
to Elohim    to you    to be

אֲנִי יְהֹוָה אֱלֹהֵיכֶם׃
your Elohim    ihvh    I

המפורש שם הם אלה יוצא ני אלה

| | | | | | | | |
|---|---|---|---|---|---|---|---|
| והו | מבה | ללה | ההע | מהש | ולו | ייי | לבח |
| מבה | לאו | חהו | מלה | ההו | אכא | ללי | אני |
| ארי | ירד | ושר | לכב | לוו | ויר | נאו | סיט |
| הבר | לאו | עשל | האא | מהל | פהל | ירד | עלם |
| ראנ | אום | דרי | ריי | שאה | ריי | ילה | נאל |
| יינ | נהי | ייי | טום | עשל | מיכ | מבה | הרי |
| אכא | דרי | מנק | לכב | אדע | ייו | ירו | יחי |
| החש | מקד | זיי | ושר | ייל | עמם | ילי | מום |

93874419R10044